Can't Get It Right, But Trying

M.L. Ginn

United States:
10 9 8 7 6 5 4 3 2 1

About the Author

M.L. Ginn, 42, was born and raised in Brooklyn, New York and now resides in Newark, New Jersey. She attended Boys and Girls High School as well as the College of New Rochelle. She is the mother of one son, KT, who she spends every waking moment working very hard for. She is a medical secretary by day, but at night, she is dedicated to fulfilling her dreams. She created a t-shirt line called Melanin Monroe. She then went on to publish a mobile game app called Bubble Blast Deluxe, which debuted in the Google Play Store, but M.L.'s biggest accomplishment yet was the completion of her first memoir—*Can't Get It Right, But Trying*.

She is also the CEO of her own publishing company KT 765 Publishing, which was named after her son and the number of the building she grew up in.

Facebook: KT765Publishing
Twitter: @ KT765Publishing

Can't Get It Right, But Trying

M.L. Ginn

Dedication

I dedicate this memoir to my mother Nette, who god allowed me to spend the first 30 years of my life with before he called her home. She is the reason I learned what struggling was about early in life and the reason why I now know the true definition of hustling and doing what you have to do, no matter what to make ends meet for your family. She gave me tough love, and I did not understand it when I was a kid, but I get it now. To my little sister Jasmin, who I always treated more like a daughter, I hope I have been a decent role model to you so far. If I have not, just know that I tried and will continue to keep trying even when I'm talking crazy to you. To my grandpa Ran and Grandma Sarah, if it were not for you people, we would have been living in a cardboard box at some point during our struggles. I can never thank you enough for everything that you have done. We are blessed because of you two. I love you with all my heart and soul. To my son, KT aka my mini me, when I think about life, all I can do is picture you inside of my head. I do not know who I would have been if I was not your mother. For a long time, that seemed to be the only thing that I thought I did right in this world. Even when you get on my nerves, I do not really go too crazy on you because in the blink of an eye you can be taken away from me the way this world is today. You are my everything! To my uncle Tony, you are the reason that I love sports. I will always remember when you would say a baseball player's first name, and I had to say the last name until I had all the famous ones memorized. My mother couldn't have asked for a better brother. I love how protective you were over us and Grandma told me that's how Mommy was over you. I love you very much. To my god brother Isaiah, you always been more like a son to me, and no matter how far apart we are from each other, I will always be there for you. To my significant other Reggie, you drive me crazy, and sometimes, all I can do is laugh about it because we have been through a lot together. Only love can make me stick around to see what else this relationship has in store for me, or maybe, I'm just crazy. Either way, I love you. I have a long list of friends who I would like to thank, but I am afraid to name them because if I dare miss one, I know I will be getting cursed out for a long time. To all my close friends, I just want to say thank you sincerely because we have been together through thick and thin, and many of you have been damn near second parents to KT. I love you all!

Chapter One

When I was 14-years old, it was very stressful. It was the summer of 88, and I was at an awkward stage in my life, fighting the battle of acne and losing off and on. Thank goodness, my slim and toned body made me look great in spandex though. I considered myself for the most part a pretty, young thang. The most stressful part of my life was trying to keep my wardrobe up-to-date and making sure the boys were checking me out when I walked the streets of Brooklyn. There was a lot of competition out there, so I had to stay on point. I had to keep up with the latest doorknocker earrings, the biggest Jamaican bangle bracelets with the prettiest rubies and stones, and I couldn't forget about the double-heart, name, or initial rings with two, three, or four on each finger. Every now and then, I would get the urge to get a gold cap and always made sure to get a different design on the tooth so I could be real fly. My hair was another big issue of its own. One month, I would want box braids, and the next month, I would want my hair to be like every chick I had seen in rap videos. I did every cut, color, weave, extension, finger waves, or scrunch hairdo that was out. Amen! The press and curl had to be put to rest.

School was never a priority to me because I had the attitude of a fool. I never felt the need to push myself to that extra limit. My motto was if I got a 65 or 70 as a grade that meant that I passed. I never thought that a high GPA would make me a better person anyway. I had very smart friends but having fun was more important to me. As a teenager, I worried about the usual stuff—boys, clothes, jewelry, and parties. When you live in the hood, that's what matters most especially if you've never been exposed to anything else. I spent my teenage years thinking that my image was everything. I wasn't too sure on how far my brain would take me, but I figured that at least I had track and field to fall back on. Unfortunately, due to a knee injury that dream ended during my sophomore year of high school.

I will never forget the day it happened. I was running in a meet in the Bronx near Van Cortland Park in the fall of 89, and I suddenly felt a pop. I slowly fell to the floor, and when I tried to get back up, I realized that I couldn't straighten my leg. I had to hop off the track with my coach looking at me in pure disgust. I had no clue what happened to my knee, and she didn't even care to check on me. She was pissed because I obviously didn't win the race. After the event was over, she didn't even offer me a ride home, which was insane since we lived in the same building. Thank God for my teammates because they pretty much carried me for blocks to the train station. I had to call my grandfather to come and pick me up. Some of the kids were nice enough to stay with me until he showed up because it was dark outside.

When I got home, my grandmother and mother were pissed off. My grandmother went to my coach's house, but she wasn't home, so she slipped a nasty note under her door. I don't know what it said, but by the time I got back to school, she was very apologetic because she saw me with crutches and realized how bad the situation really was.

I loved track so much that I still get teary-eyed watching women's track and field on television. I believe that if I would've went to the right doctors, I would've had a simple knee scope surgery and would have only missed one year of running. I was told by the doctor that I have torn ligaments. Being that my grandmother felt that I was too young for surgery anyway, I knew that was definitely the end of my career. After spending over a month trying to walk without a limp, I had to start focusing on other things. I was very depressed from that because high school was the last place anybody wanted to be with a disability. Nobody really noticed that I had a limp because it didn't show much when I walked slow.

After my injury, I started putting more focus on my schoolwork. Unfortunately, boys started to become a new focus of mine as well. I had a lot of cute boys in my classes, but they were immature in my opinion. Being that I was never one to play silly games, it only made sense for me to go after the older boys. I never really saw the senior high school boys acting silly because some of them were too damn old to be in high school anyway. The average 12th grade guy was between 17-20 with full beards and mustaches. Some of them were even fathers. They didn't need a bus pass to get to and from school since most of them had their own cars. Now that's what I was talking about! There was only one problem. I looked and dressed too young. The simple solution to all of that was to just buy tighter clothes, stick my butt out, and strut a little harder when I passed them in the hallway. To my surprise, my plan worked as desperate as it sounds.

The first one who stopped to give me attention was a thug with a cute face named Greg, so I couldn't refuse. The first thing that I learned about older guys was that they are about less talking and more action. That was a big problem for me. I was all talk and no action. Naturally, I knew it would be a short-lived relationship. I had no time to waste, so I moved on to the next one. The next guy I started talking to was a little younger than my ex but just as mature. His name was Dave. He was so smooth and soft spoken, so I felt like he might've been the right one to go all the way with if I had to. He made me feel comfortable enough to go to his house, during school hours of course, to see if we could get it on. As we sat on his couch acting all weird and awkward around each other, we finally gathered up the courage to kiss. We kissed for a very long time, and then he stood up and took my hand, leading me to his mother's room. She had a bigger bed than he had, so I guess he was trying to impress me. We went back to kissing, and without any extra foreplay, we got straight to business. It didn't feel as good as the chicks in those pornos made it out to. While he was pumping his life away on top of me, I decided to make the best of the situation and started to participate. I was unaware that my participation was supposed to be with my body, so I started making noise just like the porno chicks. I got louder and louder until it was over. What a fucking disaster! He never messed with me again because he said that I couldn't handle him and he didn't like screamers. Thanks a lot to all the stupid chicks in the flicks whom I thought I had learned something from.

Chapter Two

The remaining years of high school were filled with trying to pass classes and experimenting with more boys. No one turned out to be 'boyfriend material', so I started looking outside of school. The sad part about my struggles in school was that I had completely given up on my future goals. After my knee injury, I didn't want to go to college anymore because I wanted a track scholarship, and I couldn't depend on my grades since they were so average. Then I thought that I wanted to become a nurse, but my math and science skills told me that wouldn't be easy either.

I had a lot of stuff going on outside of school that caused me a great deal of stress too. I had a lot of responsibilities at home. My grandparents moved to the south in the fall of 89 after my grandpa retired from his job. He was a mailman, and everybody loved him. He was the type of mailman who would deliver your check no later than 11 a.m. so you could head out early to cash it and run your errands. It was very difficult for me to see them move away, being that we all lived in the same house together. I wanted to go with them, but they didn't think that it would be fair to take me and leave my little sister behind with my mother. I remember the day they left to drive to their new home as if it was yesterday. It was a beautiful afternoon. I walked them to the parking lot, and when they got in the car and drove off, I honestly felt my heart stop for a second. That was a hurt that took me a long time to recover from. They were more than just Grandma and Grandpa; they were my everything. I used to hang out with my grandmother more than I did my mother. My mother and sister were road dogs.

As I got older, I began to help my mother out with her babysitting business. I had to pick the kids up from school and sometimes babysit for her when she had business to take care of. Sometimes, I felt like those kids were mine because I spent so much time with them. Helping my mother out took away from a lot of fun I should've been having as a teenager. Having that type of responsibility definitely made me grow up way too fast and made me a little resentful towards my mother. My home duties took a lot out of me mentally because she depended on me too much, but what could I do? How do you tell your mother no? I was determined to make sure that if I ever had children, I would never burden them with my responsibilities.

Every chance that I had to get out of the house, I made the best of it. I needed to feel free, and whatever it took to do it, I was down. Sometimes, my friends and I would ride the train to nowhere or just walk back and forth to the store and take as long as possible doing it. I would go to the corner store for my mother and make sure that trip would take at least an hour. That kind of fun wore out really fast though. In mid-July of the boring summer of 1990, life as I knew it was about to change. There was a party set for one Saturday night in the Community Room. This was the biggest event of the summer and my first big party. I had a curfew set for 12:30 a.m. which really meant 1 a.m. or whenever my friends went home. There was no way I was going in the house first and risk missing some action.

The dress code for the party was spandex for the girls. Spandex was right up my alley being that I had runners' legs. My crew and I wore different color spandex and jelly sandals. I even sprayed some burgundy hair coloring over the front of my hair to match my shirt. When we got to the party, we were so hyped because the music was good, and there were tons of people in attendance. There were also older guys there from my complex, so I knew that it was going to be a good night. The DJ played all the hottest rap music, and everyone was partying hard, but then the night took a strange turn. Somebody turned all the lights out, and the DJ started playing reggae music. All the guys were grabbing chicks up so they could slow wine them up against the wall. The whole scene was dark and steamy with the air filled with smoke. This guy named Bee grabbed me to slow grind up on, and being that he was five years older than me, I was ready to let him get up on it. This was my first real dance with a guy, and it was the best feeling I ever had in my life at that time. He was holding me real tight from behind and while grinding up on me, he was feeling all over my body. I was nervous, scared, and horny all at the same time. He went as far as to put his hand inside my panties and started caressing my little love button. I didn't know what to do, so I let him touch me while we were grooving to the reggae music. Then somebody turned the lights back on, and everybody saw us dancing with his hand in my drawls. I was so embarrassed, but when I got home, I slept like a baby after such a great night out.

That's when the love affair began with my future baby daddy. Ugh! He was a cool dude in the beginning of our relationship. I loved that he was older than me and very book smart, but what I loved more was the idea of having a grown man's attention. I used to brag all the time to my cousins about how I had a man with a good paying job. I was only 16, so I was easily impressed. He used to buy me stuff all the time and give me money. At that point, he could do no wrong in my eyes, but in the end, he turned out to be a liar and a manipulator. I had a really hard time trying to focus on my schoolwork, and he didn't make it any easier. Since my knee injury kept me off the track team, I lost all interest in school, and Mr. Manipulator used to bribe me to stay home. He would offer me a home cooked breakfast and money that was equivalent to a day's pay, and I accepted it of course. We had lots of fun together playing house and him teaching me more about the birds and the bees. He wasn't my first experience, but he was my first real lover, and I knew he was supposed to be the one. He took such good care of me that I didn't have to ask my mother for anything anymore. I got my lunch money, hair money, clothes, shoes, and jewelry from him. Having a man didn't seem that bad. It kept me out the street, which also kept me out of trouble. I went from making trips to the corner store with my friends for junk food 20 times a day to going out with my man for steak dinners.

Chapter Three

In just one year, things got very serious and could only have gotten better, so I thought. I spent every day with Bee and got very attached. We saw each other seven days a week and had sex all seven of those days. At the time, life was going great, but then the unimaginable happened. I missed my period. At 17-years old, I knew I shouldn't have been missing my period. Every morning, I felt sick and severely nauseous. I tried to convince myself that nothing was wrong, but it wasn't working. I wanted to be many things in this world but pregnant was definitely not one of them. I walked around for months trying to ignore a situation that wasn't going away. I had let too much time go by, and I knew that I had to make a decision. I was messing up in school, and the last thing I needed was to have a baby. I was too embarrassed to tell a soul, but I decided to terminate the pregnancy, and he had my back. Besides, he was 22-years old and should've been a little more responsible for his actions.

There I was all young, dumb, and misinformed. I sat down, looked through the *Yellow Pages*, and found a clinic. Naturally, I had to find a place in the city because there was no way in hell I was going to a local clinic and risk bumping into anybody I knew. I finally picked a place and called to find out what I had to do to fix the mess that I had made. I totally blamed myself for getting pregnant because

I knew better. I just didn't have the sense or the balls to tell Bee to use a condom.

"Do I have to bring a parent?" I asked the clinic's receptionist.

"No."

"Do you take Medicaid?"

"Yes."

Thank God! I thought to myself.

"When was your last period?"

After telling the woman how long ago it was, she told me that it was almost too late for me to have an abortion, and I had to come in soon. She also told me that I had to have a two-day procedure to get rid of the baby. That had me terrified, but I made my appointment ASAP.

As Bee and I were on our way to the city the morning of my appointment, he got a phone call that his first nephew was just born. That made me feel like an even bigger piece of shit. How ironic was it that a life had just come into this world and one was being destroyed at the same time. The whole experience was very eye opening because I was so far along in my carelessness that it took two days to undue this mess. Day 1 was to do paperwork and meet with a counselor to discuss how many weeks along I was and if I was sure about my decision. I was almost five-months pregnant, and I was certain that I wasn't ready to have a baby.

I went into a freezing cold exam room and undressed from the waist down. The next step was very uncomfortable for me as I laid on the exam table and placed my feet in the stirrups. They placed a bunch of sticks inside of me to open up my cervix. They told me that my cervix needed a day to open up and then they could remove the fetus. The procedure was very painful. I went home with very bad cramping, but that's what I deserved. The next morning as we were on our way back to the office to finish the procedure, I wasn't quite sure how I should've felt. The only feeling that I could come up with was one of stupidity. I felt stupid for letting this happen and not talking to anyone about it, stupid for not telling my mother, and stupid for waiting so long to have the abortion.

It was a beautiful day in May, right before Memorial Day weekend, and I knew I had a bright future ahead of me to think about. I was determined not to cry because crying is simply not in my nature. I had to own up to my mistakes and move on. After waking up in the recovery room, I felt sleepy but a whole lot better. The craziest part about when I first opened my eyes was looking to my left and seeing one of my relatives a few stretchers away. I was praying to God that I was seeing things, but I wasn't.

I was just trying not to feel guilty about doing that to an innocent baby. Why did he or she have to suffer like millions of other babies because of stupid people like me and Bee? This had to be the most selfish act a woman can do, and I promised myself that I would never do it again. Bee's usual way of handling a bad situation was to spend money. Shopping was the cure for all his problems. The first thing we did when we left the clinic was head over to Midtown. A sundress and a pair of jeans boosted my spirits just a little bit. Then we took a walk to a few shoe stores, and he bought me a pair of sandals. I loved the gifts, but it wasn't satisfying me like I thought it would. I couldn't erase what had just happened that morning out of my head. I knew deep down inside that it was the right thing to do, but I still felt like a murderer. Since I was always good at hiding my feelings, I planned to walk in my house with a smile on my face as if nothing ever happened.

When I got home, I had to keep myself busy, so I cleaned the entire house. I even rearranged the furniture. I pushed and pulled the sofa until I felt like I made a difference. I almost dislocated my shoulder, so I stopped and quickly sat my ass down. I sat there and daydreamed for a little while about my 18th birthday coming up, and that made me smile just a little bit. Then reality hit me again, and I started thinking about school and how I messed everything up and wouldn't be graduating on time.

It was towards the end of the school year, and I was very behind with my grades. Since I loved working every summer, I refused to entertain the idea of going to summer school. I knew that it wasn't the best decision, but the only way I was going to get any new jewelry or sneakers for school was if I worked. I loved the fact that Bee always bought me stuff, but I wanted the chance to buy something with my own cash. The summer flew by very fast, and the time had come for a new school year. I knew that I had a lot of work ahead of me. My life just wasn't the same since I tore the ligaments in my knee and replaced my track career with boys. I promised myself to get focused and try to make up for lost time.

When the first day of school came, it was nice to see that everybody had made it safely through the summer. Of course, most of the dudes had tons of war stories. They talked about who had beef with who and all the other bullcrap they yapped about. As the teacher gave out the program cards, a lot of people were comparing classes to see who they would be hanging out with for the day. The other half of the class was pissed off because their programs said *See Guidance Counselor* down the entire page. After that day, I never saw those folks again. I found out that they were all kicked out because they were 18 and older with too little credits to graduate any time soon, so they transferred to alternative schools. That scared me, and I kept my fingers crossed that the year would go well. My grades weren't that bad but definitely could've been better. The biggest problem was just passing midterms and finals. I struggled a lot, but in the end, I passed the test; it was pure luck every time. I could never focus on studying because I was always worried about everything else going on in the world but my own business. Plus, my other distraction was my mother developing health issues and me worrying about her. She was constantly on my back about finishing high school. That was really important to her because she didn't finish after giving birth to me.

I was really struggling, but I never told anyone. My mind wasn't right, and I didn't know who to talk to. I couldn't seem to buckle down and get serious about my schoolwork again. I was too distracted by having a boyfriend. All I wanted to do was hang around him and nothing else. As soon as I was home from school, I did everything that I needed to do for my mother, and then I waited patiently for Bee to get home from work. I spent most of that school year struggling to catch up, and had I not been around him so much, I believe I would have tightened up and aced all my classes. Mommy didn't care if it took me ten years to finish just as long as I finished. Even though I could've caught up faster if I went to summer school, she wanted me to continue working during the summers so I could stay in the habit of making my own money. I did the same thing every summer with my paychecks—went shopping for school clothes.

After a few months into school, I didn't have the energy that I usually had, and my period was late…again. I noticed that every time I brushed my teeth, I would gag when the toothbrush touched my tongue. I didn't like the feeling, and I hoped to God that I wasn't pregnant again. As soon as I would get to school for my first period class, I would park my ass down in the back-corner seat and take a nap. That was all I could do every day, all day. Physically, I was in school, but mentally, I was in my bed. The fifteen-minute train ride was horrible because of the movement of the train. It made me want to vomit. There was no doubt in my mind that I was pregnant. At that point, I didn't go to the doctor, but I knew the signs and symptoms, and my period was still missing in action. *Damn! Why? Why?* Stupidity, that's why. Careless, that's why.

I told my loving boyfriend that I missed my period and thought that I was pregnant. His response was, "Yes!" I should've known something was wrong with him from that point. Honestly, he never really worried about the right shit. He liked giving me money to miss school for the day. He brought me gifts when I was mad at him, and he liked to obsess over my body. He loved my shape. He could care less about how smart I was and how well I did in school. All those things I never noticed in my immature years of life. What grown man wants their teenage girlfriend to have a baby? I was walking around for months without going to the doctor and tried to act as if nothing was happening. At that same time, my body was slowly changing. My mother kept asking me questions like why was I sleeping so much? Then she started asking me if she could borrow a few "sanitary napkins" as she called them. My answer was always that I ran out or didn't have enough to spare. My explanation for sleeping too much was that I had a hard day at school. I stopped going outside to hang with my friends and went to bed as soon as I got home from school. My mommy wanted to have a sit down with me. She told me that she noticed how much time I was spending with Bee, and she didn't want me to get pregnant. She offered to take me to get birth control pills. Lord, have mercy! Why didn't she say that to me before then? Shit, why didn't I ask her before then? Obviously, I chose the cowardly way out and said that I didn't need the pills because I wasn't doing anything. That was probably a good time to tell her I was already pregnant. I was on a definite losing streak. I had no plans, and Bee and I were the only two who knew what was going on. He was so happy and couldn't wait to tell his mother, but I told him that he couldn't tell her if my mother didn't know. I made him hold out for four months until one night he decided to put my back against the wall and threatened to tell if I didn't. Unfortunately, I knew he was right. I shouldn't have been walking around with such a big secret.

The next evening was sure to be the night that I told my mother. That was definitely the most difficult conversation that I ever had to have. After 8 p.m., I watched every hour pass by, but the words couldn't come out of my mouth. By midnight, I said eff it and went to bed. I decided to tell her the next day, but my dilemma wouldn't allow me to rest well. I woke up at 4 a.m., and since I couldn't fall back asleep, I figured I had to tell her. It was either tell her then or else she would find out when the baby was ready to come out. I sat on the edge of her bed while she slept, still working on my approach in the meantime.

A half an hour had gone by, and I was just sitting on the bed like a dumbass. I was so mad at myself that I decided to just do it. I turned her TV on and then I tapped her leg three times, hoping to wake her up.

"You up?" I asked as she stirred a little.

"Yeah...why?"

15

"I'm-I'm-I'm…uh," I said, trying to get it out, but instead, I froze.

"Are you pregnant?" she finally asked me. I nodded my head. "You serious?"

"Yes."

"Oh, my God, your grandmother is going to kill me."

"Why?"

"She didn't want you to stay in the city after she moved down south, but she knew that it wouldn't be right to leave your little sister behind to grow up without you."

Later that morning she called my grandmother, and sure enough, my mother got the cursing of the century. Grandma ripped her a new one.

"Thanks a fucking lot," she said as they got off the phone. I wanted to laugh, but I knew better. The only thing I could do at that moment was apologize. None of this would've ever happened if I would've just kept it real and admitted to my mother that I was having sex. I could've easily gotten on birth control.

Since my secret was out at home, I figured that I could tell everyone at school, but I quickly decided against it. I was too busy playing innocent to let them know I was pregnant. I was just too ashamed. I knew lots of teenage mothers, and nobody judged them as far as I knew, but I felt like it wouldn't be the same for me.

Chapter Four

My mother took me to my first OB appointment in January of 1993, and I found out that I was four months pregnant. My baby was due on June 30th. I was very upset with myself for waiting so long to go to the doctor, but I could finally sleep in peace knowing that I wasn't hiding anything anymore. Towards the final months of my pregnancy, my loving boyfriend who used to spoil me rotten was changing his ways as fast as I began gaining weight. The only thing that he seemed to be thrilled about was that we were having a boy.

Since I was home, I wanted to start picking up the things that I would need for my son. After making my shopping list, I forgot the most important thing—money. Bee was being tight with his all of a sudden, and all the gifts and the shopping just stopped. I knew I couldn't get a job so far along in my pregnancy, so to keep tradition alive, my mother took me down to the welfare center, had me taken off her case, and made me apply for my own. The process was total bullshit. They give you an envelope full of papers that you don't care about reading and annoying questions to answer. The application approved me for cash, food stamps, and health insurance for me and my baby. This was very embarrassing for me, but I had no other choice. Bee had absolutely no sympathy for me and wouldn't help me buy anything. If it wasn't for my two baby showers I had given by his mother, my mother, and good friends, my baby wouldn't have had a thing. He was really turning into a piece of shit. He stopped spending quality time with me when I really needed him by my side. It was as if I meant nothing to him anymore.

The evening of Valentine's Day, he came to my house and handed me an ice cream cake, a teddy bear, and a card. Before I could even lock my door and go sit down to talk to him, he kissed my cheek and walked right back out. I guess he was spending Valentine's Day with the one he really loved. Whenever I would ask him to come and see me, he wouldn't because he was too busy hanging with his homies or whoever the hell he wanted to be around. I was at a lost on how to keep him interested in me or why he even lost interest to begin with. I tried to find ways to get him to hang around me more, but nothing worked. I used to cook all his favorite meals, I would have sex with him even though I didn't want to, but that only kept him around temporarily. As I began the countdown 'til the day my son was to be born, I was gaining weight rapidly, and it was not a pretty sight. My last couple of weeks was horrible. I was fat as hell with a huge nose, swollen feet, and a black neck. I had reached the point where I had to go to the doctor once a week to check on the baby. The only thing that the nurses would say to me after checking my weight and blood pressure was to watch my salt intake. They never warned me about the damage that I was doing to myself, and to be perfectly honest, I never asked either.

One month before I was due to deliver, my grandmother on my father's side was admitted to the hospital and died not that long after. We all called her Nana. She was very sweet and funny as hell. She used to cook some really good salmon cakes and whatever else her grandkids wanted. She also cursed like a sailor, and I loved to hear every bad word that came out her mouth. I hated that she wasn't going to meet my baby. I will never forget how she looked at her funeral because it was the first time I ever saw someone lying in a casket with a smile on their face. I guess that meant she was in good hands, but it sure hurt to see it.

I was hoping that my baby would be born on my 19th birthday, but when my birthday came, I didn't feel like I was anywhere near ready to pop. On June 25th, I went for my regular weekly clinic appointment, and as usual, I had gained even *more* weight. That put me at 206. Before my pregnancy, I only weighed 135 pounds. Not going to school or having anywhere to go left plenty of reason for me to eat constantly. My biggest problem was my salt intake. I would eat canned goods, fried foods with extra ketchup, and barely ate a fruit or vegetable. I remember eating a whole box of cereal in one sitting all because I didn't want anybody else in the house to have any. Now that's being a true fat-ass.

After waiting for over an hour to be seen by the doctor, I was very agitated from waiting so long. The random doctor on rotation for that week wasn't that nice like the one from the week before. When you are a clinic patient, you don't get the luxury of having one doctor assigned for your care. As he reviewed my chart, he started explaining to me that my blood pressure was very high, and they couldn't let me go home like that. I didn't understand what the problem was because it was high every time I came in, and no one ever made a big deal before. When I asked the doctor how high it was, he said it was 180/90. He also told me that I had preeclampsia. This is what happens when you are young, dumb, and don't listen to anybody. My stupidity could have led to me having a seizure, stroke, heart failure, or even water in my lungs. The bottom line was I could've killed my baby and myself. The doctor told me that I had to be admitted to the hospital to be monitored. I got upset because I was at the appointment by myself with no bags or any money in my pocket. Since Bee was at work and my mother was at home doing her babysitting business, I was stuck to deal with the situation by myself. The room that they took me to was cool because it was a single, and I wanted to be alone anyway. The girls who were in labor across the hall were screaming and hollering in pain. It didn't take me long to realize that I was not ready to deal with that drama for myself. I called my mother to let her know that I had to stay and to get there as soon as possible.

There I was on a lovely Friday afternoon laying in a hospital bed alone in the dark with a monitor strapped to my belly checking my baby's heart rate. I was told that keeping the lights off in the room would help to keep me calm and help to control my blood pressure. The doctor told me that they wanted to induce my labor for the safety of my baby and me because my pressure wasn't dropping. Hours later, it was raising even more because the medication they used to induce me wasn't working. There were different doctors checking me constantly, and it was pissing me off. One of the doctors told me to relax while he placed two fingers inside me, but I couldn't.

"Well, it's not the first time something has been in there, so just relax," he said.

"The difference is that you are a stranger, and I'm not used to having strange fingers inside of me, so to get the fuck out of here."

As the hours began to go by, I started getting really bad cramps but no real labor pains. My cervix wouldn't open up past four centimeters, and that meant that my baby wasn't trying to come out. Once the morning came, they checked my pressure again, and it was still high. I didn't dilate anymore, and the doctors decided that I had to have an emergency C-section. Bee and my mother were there but had to step out while I was prepped for surgery. To make matters worse, they sent an elderly nursing assistant in the room to shave my private area. The lights were still off, and her hand was shaking. Hell no!

As her hand continued to shake with the razor in it, coming towards my sacred box, I said, "Miss?"

"Yes, baby?" she said.

"Get out!"

She didn't even argue with me. She just packed up her magic kit and got the hell out of my room. Then a nurse came in and told me to take off all my jewelry, nail polish, and the hair pins out of my head.

"Hold up! I can't take my hair pins out…it's holding up the hair for my French roll."

After my tantrum, I took my pins out and made Bee hold them in his pocket. Then the doctor came in and was ready to give me my epidural. Lord, it was the biggest needle that I had ever seen, but I took it like a champ because the doctor told me that one wrong move while that needle was going inside, and I would never walk again. He didn't have to tell me twice. A few minutes later, I felt numb from the waist down so that meant that it was time to go into the operating room. My mother was very upset she couldn't be there, and they told Bee that he couldn't come with me because he wasn't my husband. Again, I was going through this whole thing alone.

As they rolled me into the operating room, I felt like the star of a real small Broadway show with all the bright lights and instruments. Since my legs were numb, they had to move me from my bed to the operating table. I felt bad for them because I was 206 pounds of dead weight. I was very scared because I was surrounded by strangers, and the way they strapped my arms down didn't help one bit. I just laid there staring at the bright lights with tears rolling down my face. As far as I knew, my blood pressure was definitely high enough for my baby to be born on the same date as my death. Those minutes right before you think you're about to die are unforgettable. I started thinking about how much better I wish I utilized my time in school. *Why didn't I pay attention in math? Why didn't I graduate on time? Why did I end up at a hood doctor to treat my knee? Why did I not go away to college? Why did I have to be a backup babysitter for my mother? Why? Why? Why?* The nurses put a blanket over me to block me from seeing below my breasts. They gave me something through my IV that had me in a daze, and then they were ready to cut me open. I felt them cutting me across my stomach from left to right; it felt like a finger moving across my skin. Thank goodness for that epidural. I felt some tugging and pulling, and a few minutes later, my son was out. Then I heard him cry for the first time after they slapped his little butt.

The room suddenly turned into a complete blur as they brought him close up to my face and asked me if I could see him. I said, "Yes." The truth was all I really saw was a brown face, but I was too afraid to tell them because I didn't want them to put some shit in my eyes and I ended up blind. The face I really envisioned was actually my friend Kelly's baby who was just born a few months before. Right after that, I fell asleep. When I woke up again, Bee was standing there with a smile on his face. He was hyped up because his first-born was a boy, and he was born on the day of some popular beach festival in Long Island. We didn't talk much because I was very groggy. I just remember yelling at him because I felt like my legs were sliding off the bed, and I wanted him to put them back. He kept telling me that he put them back, but I couldn't feel his hands touching me. I just started crying because I thought I was paralyzed. The next thing I knew, I fell back asleep. The next time I woke up, Bee was standing there again but with different clothes on. I was very upset because I thought it was a whole new day. He just started laughing at me. He went out, celebrated the birth of his son, and came back as if nothing happened. I really wasn't interested in seeing him all happy while I felt so miserable. All I wanted to do was see my son, but they wouldn't let me because I had a very high fever. That meant that I couldn't hold him or feed him. All I could do at that point was go back to sleep. They told me that I would have to be on a liquid diet for a couple of days and taught me how to hold a pillow to my stomach and cough, so I wouldn't bust the staples they had put in. The whole weekend was a complete blur. I had no sense of time. I don't think my baby had a name for at least two days. I couldn't come up with anything for him. The only names that I could think of were the names of people who I already knew, so we went with his father's suggestion. We called him KT, and he is absolutely the best thing that has ever happened to me.

Chapter Five

KT weighed 7lbs 8oz. and was 19 ½ in. long. The hospital kept us for a week because they claimed that I had a fever every day for five days straight. I thought they were just trying to bill the shit out of my insurance and used me as the excuse. They had me on a liquid diet, which was the worst. These days, a liquid diet would sure do me and a few other people some good though. Finally, when the seventh day came, I was so happy to go home with my son to start our new lives together. Since Bee had to work, my mother brought us home. She had to bring me a fresh pair of clothes and KT a little outfit. As simple as this task was, of course, she had to mess my part up. She showed up to the hospital with the same clothes that I gave her to take home when they admitted me. I was so mad at her because the clothes were balled up and wrinkled, and the same panties were in there. I couldn't do anything besides laugh.

Everything was already set up at home for KT, so after sitting at home and holding him for hours, I finally stopped and laid him in his bassinet. He was a very peaceful baby and barely ever cried. The only thing that would upset him was changing his diaper and the initial feeling of being placed in the bathtub. After like a month, he realized that the bath water was his friend, and he would kick and splash away. After a bath and a bottle, he usually fell asleep right away.

Raising a baby wasn't as hard as I thought thanks to all the babysitting that I'd done against my will. My baby took lots of naps, and it gave me plenty of time for household chores. I had so much free time that I would hand wash all his clothes and scrub stains until my hands would hurt. Boiling bottles was my favorite chore. I felt so responsible knowing that my baby would have his bottle as clean as possible for his food. Being that Bee had a job and we didn't live together, he missed many precious moments. He loved to put KT on his chest so he could fall asleep. I guess that would be his 'proud papa' moment. We had lots of mommy-and-son time together for many years. I tried to give him as many memories as possible.

I decided that when the fall came around, I was going to go finish school and get my high school diploma. I went to a local young mother's school, which was close to home. When I registered myself into the school, I lied and told them that I didn't have a babysitter and used that as my reason why I didn't go back to my original high school. They didn't know my mother was a babysitter, and they didn't need to know. Since I lied, I had to take KT with me to school every day and bring him to their nursery. It was okay for the first month, but by the time he was six months, I officially realized that I bit off much more than I could chew. Between the heavy book bag I had to carry and him, I was a mess. Thank goodness, I only had to do six months because I was physically worn out.

After graduating, there was no prom or ceremony for me, but it didn't matter because I was just happy that I finished. I was also lucky enough to get my diploma from my original high school—Boys and Girls High. I spent the next year taking care of my baby and helping my mother out with her business. Once KT was potty trained at 2-years old, I decided to send him to daycare. To some people, it didn't make sense being that I had a live-in babysitter. I never wanted to take advantage of my mother, and I created a motto for myself—treat my everyday life as if I had no one around to help me. I figured that it would teach me to be a responsible mother and not take advantage of others, but even with that frame of mind, I always had lots of back up support when I needed it.

Once I enrolled KT in daycare, I decided to try community college. Financial aid covered the cost, and public assistance would pay for his daycare. Of course, there were a million appointments for me to bring in a million documents in order for them to pay. They definitely try to make it hard for you to get ahead. I didn't give up though because I really wanted to go to school. I owed my son and myself the opportunity at a better life. On the day of my final public assistance appointment, I turned in all my paperwork. The caseworker slowly went through everything, and as soon as she got to the part that showed what school I wanted to attend, the witch told me that it was not on their list of approved schools. It was Borough of Manhattan Community College and is a well-known community college, so how could it not be acceptable? Then she told me that I had the option of doing a work assignment that consisted of cleaning the park near my house, or I could get an office job. I decided to entertain her idea.

"I'll take the office job. How much does it pay?"

"It doesn't. That's how the childcare expenses will be covered, and you'll get work experience in the process," she said.

I really thought that woman must've bumped her damn head on her way to work because that was the dumbest shit I had ever heard in my life. All I wanted was a better life and a little bit of help temporarily, but of course, there had to be a few roadblocks. I hated the welfare system with all my heart. I quickly walked out the office. I was in a hurry for a place to cry in private. The downtown area was very busy, so between the buildings and the train station, I had nowhere to hide. The feeling to cry was so overwhelming that I caught a huge lump in my throat, my head began to hurt, and my eyes started to fill up with tears. I fought and fought but couldn't hold them back any longer; the tears started rolling down my face. I couldn't believe that I lost control like that in the street. I quickly got myself together and wiped my face. I made myself a promise to try to do better on my own. I decided to enroll in school anyway and let KT stay with my mother since it was only for a few hours twice a week.

Classes started out okay, and the homework was easy. The only problem that I had with school was not having enough money to actually get there. I was barely making it there and back, so I had to forget about having lunch money. Every now and then, I would have a dollar to spare. I found a little coffee shop near the school that sold butter bagels and a small tea for $1. Mid-way through my first semester, I was taking change out of my piggy bank to get to school and for my usual $1 meal. The hardest thing in the world was walking my broke-ass past multiple restaurants every day and being too broke to buy anything, but I would've felt worst if my son was with me. That was not what life was supposed to be about. It was getting harder and harder to focus on schoolwork knowing that I may not be able to get there the next day. One would think that life wouldn't have been so rough with a working baby daddy, but that wasn't the case. He never gave me a dime for school, and he did the bare minimum for his son.

By the end of the semester, I knew I was failing all my classes, and I pretty much didn't care. Being broke was consuming my every thought, and I couldn't control it. I knew it was time for a job because $109 twice a month from welfare with a child wasn't cutting it anymore. I realized that I had nothing to put on a resume, and obviously, that's not the way to get a damn job. I always had an interest in the medical field but didn't have enough faith in myself to go to school for it. With my luck, I wouldn't have had enough carfare to get there anyway. I once heard that you could get a hospital job easier if you volunteered, so I went to Brookdale Hospital and enrolled in their volunteer program.

KT was starting to get big, and I was preparing myself for the extra money that I would need to enroll him in lots of extracurricular activities. Bee was working on a few plans of his own as well. He started hinting around at the idea of moving down south. He gave me a million reasons why moving was the best decision in the world to make. I honestly think he wanted to go so he could be closer to his mother. It didn't really matter too much to me if he decided to move or not because I didn't want him around anymore anyway. I let him take away the last part of my childhood with his lies, money, and manipulation, only to end up feeling bad about myself because I had gained so much weight after having *our* baby. The only excuse for his infidelity was that he was just "bullshitting with them chicks." It was never anything serious to him. The day I knew we would never be the same again was when he asked me to stand in front of him naked. Then he took my hand and slowly twirled me around and said that he wanted the "old me" back. The old me that could never gain more than five pounds, the old me who cut off all her hair and was wearing short colorful hairstyles that only ended up destroying my hair. I never meant to gain weight while I was pregnant, but I was always alone while he was running the streets, doing only God knows what and standing me up. Those countless dinners I cooked that he never showed up to, somebody had to eat up all that food. Or maybe, it was the ice cream cake that he dropped off to me on Valentine's Day and immediately walked back out the door to go out with another bitch. Somebody had to eat the cake. He used me, and that was the thanks I got for blessing him with his first-born son. Did I really deserve to be mistreated for not staying slim? I was with him from 16-21, and it was all for nothing except for material items and sex, no real love. My real love was sent to me on the morning of June 26, 1993.

I do remember the day that I woke up though. It was a weekday in September of 95 I believe, and he came to my house to tell me something very important. He sat me down and said that he ran into an old friend downtown. They were chatting, one thing led to another at his house, and she got pregnant. It was like someone snapped their fingers, and I woke up from being hypnotized. I didn't scream, yell, or slap him in his face. I just nodded my head and said, "Okay, I'm done." He had the nerve to get upset because I was dumping him. I couldn't understand why he thought it would have went any other way. He actually fixed his black-ass lips to say that he thought he would've at least got credit for telling the truth. The only other thing I could think to tell him was that since he thought enough of the girl to talk to her, invite her over, have sex without a condom, and cum inside of her, she should be good enough to be in a relationship with. After that, I changed the subject and told him to stay at my house to spend some time with KT while I went on a job interview. He thought I was losing my mind, but for the first time in a long time, I was doing just fine. He kept telling me that I was just upset and needed time to cool off. I was really okay with the situation. The only thing that surprised me was that it took him so long to fuck up that bad. I felt like a huge weight was lifted off my shoulders. The thought of me not having to wonder and worry about what this fool was doing behind my back felt amazing.

He spent the next couple of months trying his luck with me, but I wouldn't budge. I really hated him and refused to be nice, but it didn't stop him from trying to have sex with me every chance he got. Something eventually came over me, and I decided to care only about my own personal needs. I didn't want to be sweet anymore. I wanted to be cruel to men and take advantage of them the way they took advantage of me. Of course, I started with Bee. For the next couple of months, I would only allow him to give me oral sex and never let him penetrate me. After like the third or fourth time, he tried to force himself inside of me. I said no and put up a fight, but he wouldn't take no for an answer. I turned my back to him, and he grabbed me tight from behind and pretended like he wanted to hug me. He locked his arm around my waist and started forcing himself inside my butt. It seemed like the more I fought, the further it went in. He gave one more hard thrust and was all the way in. It felt like the lights went out in the room, and all I could see was darkness. I didn't want to scream and wake KT up because his bed was right behind mine. I just cried as I felt myself slowly passing out. Before I did, he finished and started to apologize. I was beyond shocked and knew that he was officially crazy. I never told anyone and instead just put it on my list of reasons to hate him.

Chapter Six

I finally got my start date to volunteer at the hospital. I volunteered five days a week, from 9 a.m.-2 p.m., in the surgical recovery room. I had the chance to see people straight from the operating table. I was in charge of processing the patients' paperwork. I felt really important and loved every minute of it. If I could have, I would've worked a full 9-5 shift, but I had responsibilities. After working there for nine months, they started laying people off. This was the first time that I ever saw a pink slip. It was not a figure of speech. The paper that tells you that you're fired is really pink. With people rapidly losing jobs around me, how the hell was I going to get a job? The answer was I didn't. I hated to leave the hospital, but there was no future in volunteering my services anymore, so I decided to find a real job and applied for a medical receptionist position. The only problem was that I was offered a job, but the salary wasn't put on the table yet because the doctor said I had to go through unpaid training first.

For about a month, they had me in exam rooms alone with patients who were brand new to the country and spoke no English. I was taking height, weight, and doing EKGs. I was doing so well that the doctor taught me how to do pulmonary function testing. I'm sure all the above was illegal because I had no licenses or certificates to perform any of these tests on patients, but they didn't know and probably didn't care either. It must've been some kind of scam because they were being dropped off by the dozens in a van weekly. They had everything set up so they could go to the welfare office for cash assistance, food stamps, and insurance, and then to the doctor's office for their checkups. They didn't understand English and had no idea what would be done to them at the visit, and the sad part was that they were so trusting they would let you do whatever you wanted. Lucky for them that I wasn't into fondling strangers.

After about a month went by, I had to beg the doctor for a meeting to discuss my salary since he said I was doing so well. That jackass had the nerve to tell me that he would pay my carfare and buy me lunch. I thought that was really sweet at first until I asked him what would be my salary, and he said, "We can discuss that after you've worked here a little longer."

I just smiled and said, "Okay."

My number one rule when people pissed me off was to never let them see me sweat. After the meeting, I went back to the front desk and decided to learn one last pointer—how to check insurance eligibility through the machine. At 5 p.m., I got up and told the office manager goodnight. Of course, I never went back to the office again, and I kept the lab coat. Another rule of mine was to never leave somewhere empty handed. I did like being in the doctor's office dealing with patients, so I decided to search for another medical receptionist job that would actually pay me. Even though I was doing medical assistant work, I didn't have any certifications, so I signed up with a temp agency so they could help me find a job. They were really good at finding me work, and I loved the fact that I got paid weekly. It helped me put some good hospitals on my resume; however, none of the temp jobs ever offered me a permanent position. I knew I had to focus on getting a decent paying job because I didn't want to ask Bee for any money, and my mother was having a hard time keeping up with the rent. Since the apartment was put in my name when my grandparents moved, I knew I really had to help out. It was the first thing that I ever had in my name that was important.

The steady flow of temp assignments was great, and I was starting to find my own way in the world. I was able to pay for KT to go to school, help my mother with the rent, and keep food on the table. Even though I was temporarily working and my mother was getting public assistance, we still kept running into problems keeping up with the rent. One of my very last temp jobs was actually in the process of interviewing people for the very position that I was busting my ass in every day. Not once did they offer me the opportunity to interview for it. I was very insulted because the supervisor and manager were both black women. I didn't know why I thought we would stick together. I eventually inquired about the position, and they told me to submit my resume to Human Resources, knowing damn well they didn't want me. I was never given the opportunity to interview for the position. The worst part was watching other people come in. Once the position was filled and my assignment ended, the temp agency continued to find me assignments that kept money in my pockets weekly. Unfortunately, I needed more help for the times when the assignments were only set up for a day or two. Needless to say, the work helped me build a great resume. While I was on the hunt for a full-time, permanent position, I received a job offer to work at the LaGuardia Airport doing security. I had no prior experience, but I wasn't concerned about that because I personally knew the supervisor. It was a fairly easy job but not really ideal for women.

The job eventually took a turn for the worst when they switched me to the night shift. I had a hard time changing my sleep pattern, but I did what I had to do. I kept KT enrolled in daycare since I had a steady job to pay for it. The long forty-five-minute train ride home gave me the opportunity to catch a quick nap, so I could have enough energy to make it home. As soon as I got home, I had to get KT ready for school and drop him off. Then I could go home and try to get some sleep. There were mornings where I was so sleepy that I would ride the local C train home just so I could get more sleep and would never miss my stop. One particular morning as I took my nap on the train, I noticed a man who was dressed in a trench coat and sweatpants staring at all the women in my train car for a few stops and then he left. After he left, I went back to sleep. The next time I woke up, I was a few stops away from home, and the train car was completely empty. A second later, the man with the trench coat and sweatpants was back on the train, and before I could get up, he pulled his penis out and started jerking off. I was shocked and nervous at the same time. He was staring straight into the next train car, so I figured that I shouldn't move because I might get his attention. He finished his business all over the seat and got off the train at the next stop, not bothering to put his penis back inside of his pants. He simply closed his coat and kept walking like it was business as usual. I was so stunned that I couldn't even speak to people when I got off the train. I was too afraid to open my mouth because I had the urge to vomit. I was 100% positive that I would've thrown up if I opened my mouth. I had very little time to collect my thoughts and straighten up because I had to get my baby ready for school. As soon as I stepped into the house, I got him ready really fast and damn near ran to drop him off at the school. I was in a hurry to get home and get some sleep. I was desperate to erase that morning's events out of my head.

As soon as I got back home, I told my mother what happened. She was glad that nothing happened to me but was mad that I fell asleep on the train. After our brief conversation, I closed my blinds, giving my room the look of nighttime, and went to sleep. Of course, during the day, I could never make the room dark enough, but that day, I forced myself to go to sleep. After about two or three hours, my mother came into the room and woke me up to ask me if I was hungry because she made lunch. I didn't have the urge to eat, but I asked her what she made anyway.

"Franks," she said simply.

After what I told her, I was so confused at why the hell she would ask me if I wanted a frank. I was so annoyed with her for that. It took about ten minutes before she realized that I just saw somebody playing with their 'frank', so why would I want to eat one? Geesh!

"I am so sorry," she laughed.

***

Working that security job was not ideal for a woman or a single parent at that because the payday alcoholics never liked to show up for work the next day. My supervisor knew I hated to be stuck against my wishes doing a double, so he would do everything in his power to find coverage for me. He knew my bitch fit would begin immediately if he didn't. Working doubles seemed to happen more often on Saturday mornings after payday, and I think they were getting immune to my tantrums, so I had to step my game up and demand more than for just my words to be heard. I started demanding cash up front and food to eat. Everyone thought it was the funniest shit; the first time they saw the supervisor hand me $10 and some food, they got quiet. I figured that there was no reason for me to suffer because of those lazy dudes. I knew I couldn't do that job much longer because I wasn't sleeping or eating much and turned into a tyrant, but more so because I was scared that someone was going to find out that I didn't know how to drive, and that was a requirement for the job. If my secret got exposed, I would've been fired and so would've the person who hired me.

Chapter Seven

One night, it almost happened. I was sitting in my booth on the runway, and I had to use the bathroom. The protocol was to call your supervisor, and they would drive over to cover you if no one was available, and you would have to drive the car from your post. Damn! Since I've always been resourceful and creative, I decided to keep my mouth shut. My booth was pretty high above street level so only truck drivers could see inside as they drove by. After a few more cars drove by, I quickly pulled one leg out of my pants, peed on the floor, and wiped myself with a rough paper towel that scratched my ass. I pulled my pants up quick, took my bottle of water, and poured it all over the floor to wash the piss away, and then I opened the booth door and started kicking the water out. That had to be one of the dumbest ideas that I ever thought of but the best bathroom break that I ever had. The next time I dodged the bullet from my secret being exposed was when my supervisor called my post to inform me that he was driving to me next to relieve me for a lunch break. That definitely wasn't about to happen, even though I was hungry as hell and could use a quick nap. I refused, but he wouldn't take no for an answer. Once he pulled up to my post, I opened the door and told him that I wasn't hungry. He informed me that it was mandatory, but I told him that I didn't care. He wasn't tough enough to go back and forth with me, so he just said "Okay" and left. My secret was beginning to weigh too heavy on me. As bitchy as I was, I didn't want anyone to get in trouble and suffer for helping me get a job, so I started reading the Sunday Classifieds religiously and surfed the internet to find a new job. I would sometimes apply to the same job over and over again until one company mailed me a post card saying that they received my information and to not apply again. I started slowly receiving phone calls for interviews with temp agencies. They had me taking typing tests and other various clerical tests to see if I was qualified to do secretarial work. After two months, I think I was registered with at least a dozen agencies. It was a good thing that I still worked the night shift at the airport because that left my days free for interviews.

It was no secret at work that I was a witch to my supervisor. I never kept a schedule that I didn't like. When I said "no," that was usually the end of the discussion. He even tried to write me up once because my coworkers complained about me, so he explained that I couldn't refuse a schedule, and he had to write me up for being insubordinate. I refused to accept the write up. When he handed it to me to sign, I stared into his eyes and without looking, I let the paper drop out my hand into the garbage. While he sat there in shock, I turned around and walked out. The next day, he decided to call me on my day off to come into work. Since I didn't plan for it, I didn't get any sleep, and I wouldn't be able to handle working my shift and traveling for an hour and a half each way, so I told him that I couldn't do it.

"Are you telling me no?"

"Yes, I'm saying no."

"You're not allowed to tell me no."

"Well, that's too bad."

"You know I can fire you, right?"

"Not before I quit."

"If you don't come in tonight, don't come back," he said finally putting his foot down.

"Okay then, I quit." And just like that, it was over. I knew I wasn't in a position to do something like that, but I wasn't the type of person to let anyone have the upper hand on me. I knew that I had one more check coming, and I had to make it stretch in the meantime. I didn't have a backup plan, but I was going to do my best to get back on my feet.

I tried to go on as many interviews as possible from multiple temp agencies as I patiently waited for work. When my last payday finally came, for some reason, they didn't want me to come to the office and personally pick up my check, but I knew that if they mailed it to me, it wouldn't have arrived for another three days at least. The supervisor who lived close by offered to bring it to me on his way home, which was perfect. The plan was to meet him downstairs so he could pass me the check and keep it moving. When he showed up, I rushed downstairs to meet him, and he started fumbling around like he was missing something. I instantly got upset.

"I am so sorry. I must've left it at my house. If you want, you can ride with me to go get it, and I can take you to the check cashing place before I bring you back."

I was a little hesitant at first, but I figured that it didn't make any sense to turn down a car ride when I knew I would've taken a taxi anyway. He lived so close that we made it to his house in a little over five minutes. He told me his mother lived with him, so it was safe to come in and see the house if I wanted to. Situations like that are weird to me when you are a single man in your 40s living with your mother and a cat. I guess I couldn't afford to judge him since I still lived at home with my mother and was unemployed. I walked slowly into the house and didn't take one-step past the living room. The couch and chairs had plastic on them, so I knew for sure that it was his mother's house.

"Just give me one second," he said as I sat down, "You want anything to drink?"

I gave him the evil eye, and said, "No! Now, hurry up before I get mad."

"Okay," he said walking away.

A few minutes later, he came back into the living room and sat beside me, still no check in hand.

"Do you know how pretty you are?"

"What?"

"I've wanted you since the first time I laid my eyes on you."

"Can you just give me my check so I can leave?" I decided that it wasn't that serious for me to get a free ride to handle my business. At that point, I would've rather walked the dangerous streets of the hood than to deal with his shenanigans.

He still wouldn't give me my check. Instead, he dropped down on his knees in front of me and begged to eat me out. I was frozen. I never had someone beg me to let them do a sexual favor. Where I came from, men usually didn't have to beg. Shit, a lot of men didn't really want to do that anyway unless the woman was a real freak and didn't allow a dude to do no sticking before the licking.

"No, no, no, no, no," I repeated.

Finally, he stood up and apologized before handing me my check. I was so annoyed that I stormed out and flagged a cab down in the middle of the street. I had no clue what to do about this situation. Technically, he didn't touch me, and I didn't work for the company anymore, so I guess that ruled out a sexual harassment case. I had that disgusting experience on my mind for about a month, but soon thereafter, I decided to let it go and forget about it because he really wasn't a threat to me since he was in his 40s and the size of an underdeveloped teenager.

I started getting calls for temp assignments on occasions which was a relief because I was sick and tired of the little bit of money, food stamps from public assistance, and the chump change from Bee I got every month. I was also tired of being a free assistant babysitter for my mother. I never complained to her because I knew she really needed the money. Only the Lord knew what she was going through, but we never expected anyone to care. We took good care of those kids and treated most of them like family. Hell, our services included extended hours, overnights, and some weekends. She was a true hustler. She was a childcare provider; she sold women's beauty products, promoted parties, and still went to dialysis three days a week. I think that's where I got my desire to have my hand in as many pots as I could.

Chapter Eight

Inever stopped losing hope on a permanent job coming through. I worried all the time about when it would come and if it would pay enough for us to stop struggling. I finally got a call to come in for an interview for one of the best hospitals in the city for cancer. This was actually the hospital that sent me a postcard informing me that they received my resume and to please stop applying repeatedly. I was so excited that I decided to go shopping for this interview because I wanted my presentation to help seal the deal. I also added a little personal touch by putting a small diamond pendant that I got from my grandmother on my blazer and even bought a fresh new weave and put it in myself. When you're always broke, you learn how to do things like your hair and nails yourself. It was a secretarial position in the Ambulatory Care Department. The salary was pretty decent for a person without a degree, so I was hoping this was the answer to my prayers. I was scheduled to meet with the manager of the department, and I prayed all my materialistic efforts would work. The interview went really well, and it felt more like a meeting of two well-dressed ladies who admired each other's clothing and future goals in life. She gave me multiple compliments on my suit and shoes which was a plus for me. She was very well dressed herself, so I knew that I made the right decision by going shopping. She was impressed with the temp assignments that I had done but seemed to be more interested in my personal character and where my mental state was as far as my future career goals went.

"I really enjoyed meeting with you, Monique. You should hear from me soon."

Sure enough, I heard from Human Resources a week later and was offered the job. I was so happy and full of relief. I had to go in and take a typing test, which wasn't a problem because I practiced a lot at home. The next step was my physical, and then, I was all set. I didn't smoke weed, so I didn't have to worry about passing the drug test. Once everything was cleared and processed, they set me up for the orientation class. As my luck would have it, I had to know that nothing could ever work out in my favor. The day before my orientation was scheduled to start my mother had a stroke. I spent hours at the hospital with her in shock because it happened so suddenly. It just randomly happened in the middle of the afternoon. I didn't recall her blood pressure being that out of control. Maybe it could've been her walking around stressed out about personal issues, finances, or the men in her life. I was so upset because I needed to be at the hospital with my mother to figure out how to get her better and to make sure this didn't happen again. The last thing that I wanted to do was go sit in a class for days with all these excited and happy folks while I sat there hoping my mother wasn't dying. I didn't have anyone to turn to for help or to relieve me of some of this worry I was carrying around.

As the hours went by in orientation, the less I could hear and comprehend what was going on around me. The class was filled with lots of happy young people my age who were eager to move on with their careers. I, on the other hand, was just fighting to keep from crying because I wasn't prepared to deal the aftermath of how the stroke was going to affect my mother. After the first day of orientation was over, some of my new coworkers were planning on going out for drinks to celebrate, but I couldn't because I had to get back to the hospital and check on my mother.

When I arrived at the hospital, Mommy was in good spirits but very weak and tired. I knew she wasn't feeling too down because she was flipping out about how nasty the food was and how she needed some Chinese food. The hospital kept her a few days for testing and observation and decided that there was a definite need for physical therapy at home and a walker because she was very unsteady on her feet. I was happy that her speech wasn't impaired because my mother was a talker. She talked all day and all night about anything and everything. She loved to be on the phone, so when she wasn't home, she was on her cellphone. Also as a part of her discharge, they gave her 24-hour home care assistance. That was a relief because it would be difficult for me and my sister to share those responsibilities with her being a teenager. I didn't want her taking on that kind of stress anyway.

My mother's home health aides started immediately after her discharge from the hospital, so I was a little bit more comfortable with leaving her for the day to go to work. My days would now consist of dropping KT off at the daycare, going to work, picking him up, taking him to football practice, and then going home, helping him with his homework, cooking dinner, and helping my mother with whatever she didn't want the aides to do. The problem with that was she never wanted them to do anything. She would let them sit with her and watch TV, maybe even run a few errands with her, but that didn't help relieve any of my workload when I got home. They were more like her friends that she ran the streets with. She was very independent so receiving help to do her normal daily routine was very difficult for her to accept. I guess I wouldn't have wanted my quality of life taken away from me either.

The aides didn't mind doing very little because it was better for them to do less work and still get the same money. She would always tell them not to do something because her daughters would take care of it. I hated when she did that because I didn't want my sister to have to worry about these things, and I also didn't want to take on the full load by myself. My biggest issue with her aides was that they were unable to assist her with standing up and getting in and out of the tub. They were all much lighter than she was in weight, and one of the aides was at least my grandmother's age. Naturally, I had to help my mother because I was the only one who could lift her. Finally, my weight came in handy after all. Eventually, I ended up hurting my shoulder by trying to help her get around. The last thing I needed was injuries that would prevent me from working. The area that I worked in had some of the best doctors in the city, so I was able to see a really good Sports Medicine doctor named Dr. Marx who gave me a cortisone injection for the pain. I was very grateful that I didn't need surgery.

Chapter Nine

As time went by, Mommy started getting her upper body strength back, so she could lift herself up, which was good. After that, she just had to worry about getting her strength back in her legs, which was still very challenging. This forced her to have to use a walker, and for long distances, she had to use a wheelchair to be on the safe side. She hated that because she felt like it took her independence away, but we couldn't take the risk of her legs giving out and her falling in the street with an aide who couldn't help her up. Every day was such a challenge because I worried about her constantly. We were still trying to catch up on the back rent, so that was always eating at me. I had to go to court and face the music by myself and explain why I was there. The worst part was sitting with the lawyers and having them interrogate me about how much money I owed and how fast I could pay off the balance. My mother was the brains of the operation, so she would write out in advance the entire breakdown of how much we could pay and the dates they would be paid on. Then it would be up to the lawyers to agree with the payment arrangement. I hated this so much because I still had to stand in front of the judge and promise to keep the agreement. Sometimes, I had no idea if it was going to work, but I was just the puppet, and my mother was the puppet master pulling the strings. I could never worry or focus on just one thing at a time. My way of life gave me severe anxiety at times because I never knew when something bad was going to happen. When things started to go well, I could never be in the moment basking in my glory because I knew it would be short lived.

One evening, my aunt Cel called the house to tell us that my father was in the hospital and wasn't doing well, and he wanted to see all his children. My mother and father didn't really speak much, so she wasn't quite sure on how she should feel. I really wasn't sure how I should feel either because we didn't have a tight relationship. He wasn't around during my childhood but around enough for me to know who he was, but we had a mutual respect. I had enough love in my heart for him to go because being angry about his lack of support in my adult years would do absolutely nothing for either one of us. I went to go visit him alone one afternoon, and when I arrived, he was so surprised and happy to see me but was too weak to do more than just smile. I kept a smile on my face too because I didn't want him to see me looking sad. I didn't want him to know that I was hurting for him at that moment.

The first thing that came out of his mouth was "Hey, Moeski," which was what he always called me. I didn't ask him what was wrong because I didn't want to bring his spirits down.

"Hey, how you feeling?" I asked him.

"I'm in pain...but doing okay I guess. How's K?" He was more interested in asking about his grandson, which was great because it brought a ray of sunshine to a cloudy room.

He looked so weak and no longer spoke with that razor-sharp tongue that had mentally broken so many people down to pieces. I think I managed to stay with him for about two hours, and he appreciated every minute of it. Before I left, he asked me to do him a big favor and go to the vending machine and get him a really cold can of soda, and I did just that. He was too weak to open the can, so I did it for him and watched him drink that soda like it was the first thing he had to drink in days. His hand shook so bad that I thought he would drop it, but he didn't. At that point, I was getting a lump in my throat from holding in my emotions.

"You coming back?" he asked as I got up to leave.

"Yep."

"Okay," he said with a sad look on his face as I hugged him

After that, I hurried to leave. I couldn't wait to get out that room so I could break down and cry. I ran into the nearest stairwell and plopped down hard on the first step. I cried so hard that I couldn't catch my breath for a minute. I hate cancer and the pain and suffering that it brings to so many people. I wish I could've broken every cigarette that I ever saw him pick up. I was so mad at myself for every time that I went to the store for him and bought him back a pack. I know I shouldn't be blaming myself, but I felt like I had to take some of the blame.

I knew he would probably die soon. I was just glad that I had a chance to see him, so at least, he knew that I was not mad at him for anything he did or didn't do for me as a kid. A few weeks after my visit, he passed away. The crazy part was that I knew that moment was coming, but when it came, I wasn't quite sure how I should've felt. I felt bad, but for some reason, I didn't feel bad enough to cry again. Even at his funeral, I wanted to cry, but it just wouldn't happen. Despite the nature of my mother's abusive relationship with him in the past, she was totally

devastated at the service. KT was really upset because him
and his grandpa had developed their own bond. He even
drew a family portrait in school to help deal with his grief.
The picture was of all of us standing on the grass with the
sun shining brightly over us and my father laying down by
a grave. I walked him up to the casket and let him put his
picture next to his grandpa's hands and told him to say
goodbye. My mother cried really bad for days, but I
couldn't understand why because he wasn't good to her.
After a few weeks passed by, my grandmother had to help
Mommy pull it together so she could move on with her life.

"Do you want to go join him?" Grandma just straight
up asked her.

"No," she chuckled.

"Well, you better get it together," and she did. I never
asked Mommy why she could cry for a man who wasn't
good to her even though I was very puzzled about that. I
guess the saying was true that you can't help who you love.

After the funeral, I only took three days off from work
since that's all my job allowed for grievance. My job was a
very depressing place because every patient there had some
form of cancer. Some patients even had AIDS. Sometimes,
they would come in and seem to be doing well, and then
the next time you saw them, they only had days left to live.
The pediatric floor had to be saddest place in the world to
be besides the cemetery. If you spent two minutes there,
you would change your whole outlook on life. I was
literally depressed almost every day at work. To see people
here one day and gone the next was a lot to witness. Some
of the patients pretty much lost all hope, and they would sit
outside in front of the hospital smoking cigarettes while
they were getting their chemotherapy treatments through an

IV. What can you say to a person who feels like there is no more hope? Nothing.

During that time, it was hard to focus on myself or any kind of love life. Every now and then, I would manage to squeeze in a late-night episode with a "friend". Never anything serious between me and these guys, just a little fun for the night. What I liked was that they never tried to make me think there was anything else going on between us. There was a clear understanding on where we stood. There were no lies, so no one got hurt. Every situation I got myself into was never something I was forced or tricked into. Therefore, I never got my feelings hurt, and I appreciated that. I needed an outlet even if it was only for one night because I knew that the next day I would be back to my life filled with trials, tribulations, and bullcrap.

I went to court so many times that the lawyers knew my name and face. Out of a large group of lawyers from the firm, I always ended up getting the same one who was very mean and rude to me all the time. I think he got a hard-on from asking me why I couldn't keep up with the last payment arrangement that was made. Each time, I went back, they gave me less and less time to pay off the balance owed. In the meantime, my mother was working her magic by calling my grandparents and every Tom, Dick, and Harry she knew she could borrow money from. In between all of that, she was still going to dialysis three times a week.

Each time I went to court, I never knew if the judge would say no to the stipulation agreement and tell me that I had 30 days to vacate. I was reaching a point where I actually didn't care anymore about having a roof over my head or not, but I started working on a Plan B. I went to my local welfare center to ask them about shelter information.

After waiting for hours to talk with a caseworker to find out about the protocol for moving into a shelter, I was hoping for some good news. She said I could be in one for two to three years, and I would have to leave my valuables behind. She highly recommended just bringing sweat suits, black sneakers, and no jewelry. This basically meant that I would have to go shopping for plain, no-named clothes and sneakers. That was just way too much work, and it didn't come with a guarantee that I would get an appointment any time soon. I thanked the caseworker for her information and went on my way. I was so stressed out and frustrated that all I could do was just cry a little and move on because it was already time to pick my baby up from school and spend the rest of my day trying to make him happy. I never really had 'me' time because I always had to make sure I was there for my mother, sister, and son. The only 'me' time that I could pencil in for myself was when I was on the toilet, but even then, KT would be knocking on the bathroom door asking me what I was doing. I understood why some people call it the "think tank" because you can really collect your thoughts while you're sitting there. My next option for some alone time was when KT went to bed at night. That was when I could make time for my womanly needs. I never put any man before my son no matter what, which worked out well for the type of men who only did "booty call hours" after 11 p.m. I made sure KT had all the time he needed with me before I went out, and I was always back in the house before he woke up in the morning. Yes, I have done the walk of shame on an early, sunny morning many days, but I didn't care because my most important role as a mother never once got disrupted. That was the only time I wasn't worried about the rent money or anything else that stressed me out. The more my mother hustled up the money to pay the back rent and me using all my paychecks to add to it, I was completely done with the situation. With the stress of court sitting on my shoulders and my job getting more hectic, I was constantly getting to work late. Most people would say to just leave the house earlier, but I couldn't drop KT off at the daycare any earlier than I already was. I tried to get a later start time, but management said no. I explained my situation, and they asked me if anybody else could do it. I hated when someone tried to get me to put my responsibilities on somebody else. Eventually, I got written up for lateness, but at that point, I didn't even care.

Chapter Ten

It was hard enough to sit there every day and watch people die right before my eyes. One day, I saw one of my mother's friends who I knew since I was a little girl, and the sad part was I only recognized her by her eyes and her voice. Everything else about her physical appearance had changed. When I asked the other secretary what her name was to confirm my assumption, I had to go to the bathroom and cry. I was hoping to never see anybody I personally knew come through there. I couldn't even speak to her because I couldn't get myself together and didn't want to make her feel bad, but I made sure to speak to her during her next visit, and it went well. She was telling me that she was going to beat my ass for not speaking the first time, and we both laughed together because that's how I always remembered her. She was the kind of woman who had her drinks and could curse like a sailor. Every time she came in, we wouldn't talk about why she was there. We would just talk about our families and promised to keep in touch. We kept in touch a little bit, but as time went by, I stopped seeing her, and soon after that, she passed away. I felt bad that I didn't get to see her one last time to say goodbye, but I guess it was for the best.

Then I came across a childhood friend of mine who became a patient there. Every week, I felt like I had to quit because I was simply too emotional for that place. Every time my homie came in, he would still act the same with his dirty mind and crazy sense of humor. That made me feel better and partially distracted me from why he was there in the first place. As his health started deteriorating, he began worrying about his personal business being exposed. I assured him that I never saw his medical records and to not worry about that and just focus on getting better. Unfortunately, he never got better, and I made sure that I had a chance to visit him during his last inpatient stay. I was so glad that I saw him because he passed away a few days later. All of these things taught me that it's really important to take some time out of our busy lives to pay a visit to the ill because you never know if and when they will get better.

I was really getting drained from every direction that I turned. I was tired of my home situation and tired of the way my job was treating me. They wouldn't allow us to take lunch breaks because we didn't have enough staff to cover us. When we wanted to take any vacation time, they would tell us to find our own coverage. The problem with that was anybody who would cover you for your vacation would then need coverage for themselves. The whole process didn't make any sense, but that's what happens when you have terrible management. Most days, I wouldn't eat anything or I would stuff my lab coat pockets with snacks and sneak bites of cookies and candy throughout the day. The only thing I was pretty consistent with was my daily morning cup of green tea. I once read that green tea has antioxidants in it and helps fight cancer cells, so I figured I may ruin my teeth and weight with candy and junk food every day for meals, but at least, I wouldn't have cancer.

By the time I reached the one-year mark at my job, I had been to court a handful of times for the back rent, but I went out on a limb and went for child support. The attempt to get child support was a waste of time, but I figured that it was better to try than to never try at all. Since Bee lived in another state, he had to be served by the Sheriff's Department. The first time they tried, they went to the one known address that was on file and whoever answered the door said that he didn't live there anymore. The crazy thing was that he was probably the one who answered the door. The next time, I took off work to go to court. They told me that if I wanted to make sure he was served, I would have to get a picture of him and take it to another office. They were going to file the papers with his picture, so the next time, they went knocking on his door they would simply match his face and catch him. That meant I would have to take another day off to try to get this done. I spent a few days thinking about it and decided not to bother because I was probably going to end up with very little financial support or none at all. I just let go and let God find a better way for me to provide for my son.

All this crap had me desperate for an outlet. I was probably cutting off my nose to spite my face, but I was willing to take the chance. I felt like deep down inside, I was only seeking child support out of spite because I couldn't stand Bee. He was a chapter in my life that was closed completely, so I decided to be done with all aspects of our failed relationship and get rid of the hate in my heart. I figured that I should try to find some love or companionship to heal my broken heart, so I started going online once in a while checking out the chat rooms. I would go into the ones that had guys my age and lived nearby. The whole setup was really weird because people were hooking up in real life with people they didn't even see a picture of. We were making choices based on how sexy a person's voice sounded or the dumb shit they said as their opening flirt statement. After a while, I think the purpose of the site was really for a quick hook up because there was no way you could think you were finding your soul mate over the phone. Looking back on those days, that was some really creepy and dangerous shit. The funniest thing was talking to guys and hearing their stories on how they planned on hooking up with girls because they sounded so sexy, but once they saw them, they were ugly as hell. Some of them did admit to making the best of the night and having sex, and the other half used their wingmen to help bail them out of the situation by pretending that something suddenly came up and they had to leave.

One night, I had a nice private chat with this guy who lived about an hour away from me. He seemed pretty cool, but he was tired of talking to me online. He wanted to meet me in person at least once. I agreed to let him come visit me just one time. I told him that he couldn't come to my house, so I decided to meet him outside and talk by his car. As soon as he called me to say he was downstairs, I came outside and greeted him. The first thing he wanted to know was how old I was. I laughed because I told him a million times that I was in my twenties.

"Are you sure because you look like a teenager?" I thought he was joking, but he was totally serious, and then it's like he got scared. He kept looking around as if I set a trap for him. Then he told me that he didn't believe me and started questioning the neighborhood I lived in.

"Is this area full of guys who shoot people?"

"I don't know."

Suddenly, he told me he felt uncomfortable and had to leave. Needless to say, I never called his scary-ass again, and he never called me, but I was fine with that.

Before I knew it, I was back in the chat rooms trying my luck again. I started chatting with this dude named Mike. He was a nice-looking guy who was single with no kids. We didn't live far from each other, so that made it more exciting knowing that we could possibly meet up one day. He was very cool and down to earth, which was a relief. He lived in the hood, but he seemed like the kind of guy who grew up with street dudes but wasn't into any street shit. We clicked instantly and decided to meet up. He drove to my house and met me near my building. We emailed each other pictures in the past and both looked exactly the way our pictures looked. We sat in his car and talked for hours, and everything seemed perfect. I knew from the first time we met that I wanted to get with him, and he seemed to be feeling me too. We talked every day about anything and everything, and I knew that if nothing ever became of the situation that we would at least be good friends. As time went by, I started seeing him almost every weekend because after the first time we hooked up and had sex, he had a package in his pants that I just couldn't refuse. We always went to one of the hotels that was close to my house, so he wouldn't have to drive too far to take me back home. He was so sweet to me and always offered to help me financially in any way he could. Since my temp jobs weren't too steady around the holidays, I didn't think I would be able to give KT a nice Christmas that year. I had to choose between a roof over our heads or toys, and of course, the roof won. I hated to do that to my son, but I would've hated even more to be out in the cold looking for a place to stay in the middle of the winter. One evening,

Mike and I were talking on the phone about how my Christmas was going to be a disaster. I knew there wasn't a damn thing I could do about it, but he surprised me with an offer to use his credit card to buy KT whatever I wanted. I was so shocked that I had to fight back the tears because I'd never had anybody be so generous to me. It really bugged me out because I couldn't imagine a dude with no kids being so sympathetic to my situation. I told him that I couldn't use his card because I couldn't afford to pay him back anytime soon, but he told me not to worry.

After that, my feelings for him skyrocketed through the roof. I didn't think that I could ever meet anyone who was so sweet and genuine. When I went shopping, I was afraid to order too much and make him upset so I bought just enough for KT to have an awesome Christmas. Mike was my real-life Santa Claus, and I couldn't imagine dealing with anybody else. As the months went by, I started to finally pay attention to what our relationship was really about though, and I didn't really like it. I started telling him that I wanted to go out and do more than just go to the hotel. He would always come up with an excuse as to why he didn't want to go anywhere. He didn't like to go to the movies even though I had a movie theater across the street from my house. He didn't want to go out to eat because he didn't really like to eat anything that I suggested. He didn't want to take any trips because he didn't want to get on an airplane. He only wanted to have sex. As good as the sex was I wanted more out of the relationship. I wasn't even sure after a while if it was actually a relationship. We seemed more like best friends with benefits. By the time we hit the one-year mark, I was getting frustrated and bored with what seemed more to me like a situation and not a relationship. No matter what I said and how kindly I asked for us to do anything, the answer was always "no." This caused too much friction between us, and I started to distance myself from him. He made me want more from a man, but he just wouldn't give it to me. After the one too many arguments about the same thing over and over again, we took a break from each other and started dealing with other people. That was too much stress for me to take on and handle anyway. I blamed myself for trying to keep a man who didn't want to be kept, so a timeout was definitely needed.

Chapter Eleven

The court visits were getting worse each time I went. The lawyers were getting more relentless and ruthless with me. I even tried to bring KT down there with me once thinking that it would get me out of there quickly, but that particular day, I didn't see a judge until almost 5 p.m. The allowed time to pay the balances off got shorter and shorter, and it had me so stressed out that I developed acid reflux. I was so weak and numb to the thought of getting evicted that I was kind of looking forward to living in the street. I knew that I wouldn't have to worry about paying rent if I lived in a cardboard box because those are free.

I would be so sick at work from stress that I used to throw up in my mouth by accident. The reflux used to catch me off guard all the time. Sometimes, I would be sitting at the front desk helping a patient, and right before I would open my mouth to speak, I would have a mouth full of vomit. It had reached the point where I had to see a gastroenterologist. He performed an endoscopy test on me and told me that I was suffering from a hiatal hernia and needed to change some of the things I was eating that were spicy before prescribing some medication for me. He also asked me if I was stressed out, and if so, what was bothering me. I told him my job was stressing me out and my mother's health was the other factor. He told me that I should try to ask other family members to help out with my mother, and if the job was an issue, that I should try to find a new one. That all was easier said than done. I couldn't think of anybody in my family who was free to help out, and I wasn't going to ask even if I did. As far as finding a new job, I definitely considered that and was keeping my eyes open for any new opportunities.

I prayed a lot after talking to the doctor that something good was going to happen and change for the better. Of course, it didn't because not long after that, I found out that my aunt who was my father's sister was dying from cancer. This was getting to be way too much for me to handle. She was the aunt who I stayed with every weekend as a kid, and I was not ready to see her go through the motions of this illness. The worst part was that she didn't live long after she was diagnosed. She was a very brave woman because she was the only person who I've ever known to help plan her own funeral. I respected her so much for that because she actually had her funeral dress hanging on her closet door and a wig that would match her exact hairstyle that she wore every day. I don't think Auntie lived a year with her illness, and just like that, she was gone. I remembered telling my job that I had to attend her funeral and what she passed away from, and those heartless heffas asked me if I was coming in to work after the funeral. Words can't describe how pissed off that made me. I couldn't understand why they thought I would want to be in that place watching someone else be sick from that dreadful illness. I told them that I wouldn't be coming in. I knew that my days were numbered there anyway.

On one of my very last court appointments, I wanted everything to end. I wanted it to be the very last trip down there. I wanted them to say I didn't bring enough money. I wanted them to say I had to get out of the apartment. I didn't care about being homeless. I just wanted it to stop so my mother could see that it was time to let go of a place we couldn't afford. I took my time heading down to the courthouse. I knew it would be over for us if I showed up late and missed my name being called, so I put together a definite plan to end it all. After walking KT to school, I decided that I was going to go find somewhere to sit down and eat breakfast. I sat down in this restaurant near my house for two hours. By the time I started making my way to the train station, it was almost 11 a.m. I felt a sigh of relief that my mission was surely accomplished. I even took the local train to let more time go by. As I approached the court building, I didn't feel that usual feeling of possibly throwing up or shitting my pants. I felt like I stumbled upon a new beginning coming soon. Once I walked into the courtroom, I was told by the officer to not approach the desk. I had to wait until they were finished with the calendar call. I was stunned! Seriously, how the hell did I not miss the calendar call? I didn't realize that they had a 9 a.m. and 11 a.m. call and were running a little late. I've always been in the waiting room with the attorney around that time, so I never witnessed it. That meant that it wasn't over for me. *Why me? Why?* So once again, I had to sit down with the rude-ass lawyers to discuss why I didn't make my payments on time. It was the same song and dance over and over again. Another payment arrangement with another fake promise to make the payments on time.

The very next day I got to work late and was called in for a meeting to discuss my lateness. I was already in a terrible mood because I had the train ride from hell. The trains were severely delayed that morning as if I needed any more aggravation. It was so crowded that people were close enough to each other, looking like they were in relationships. I couldn't stand to be so close to people because you have no choice at that point but to smell their body odor, hot breath, or feel certain body parts. I knew I didn't have far to ride, so I just kept my forearm up to keep some sort of barrier up between me and this guy who was standing next to me. He looked like he was in his early 20s but didn't look like he was headed anywhere in particular. I knew I had to be careful before that fool tried to snatch my bag or chain. He was standing on my right side, so I was watching him from the corner of my eye. I was only on the train with him for three stops, but it felt more like ten. He was staring really hard at me, and I was starting to get annoyed because he seemed like he was so focused on my face. His eyes were big and wide and his body jerked like he caught a chill. My train stop approached, and the whole train car cleared out with me. For some reason, I decided to stop for a second on the platform to make sure I had everything and as soon as I stared down at my jacket pocket, I saw semen on it. I was in shock and froze for a second. By the time I snapped out of it, the train door closed. I was going to beat his ass with my purse since I didn't have a weapon. All I could do was wipe the mess off my jacket with my newspaper and head to work before I was any later. When I got to the job, I told the nurses what happened, and they were trying to convince me to take the jacket to the precinct to get his DNA checked. I really didn't want to talk about it, so I didn't go. My mother tried to convince me to send the jacket to the cleaners and see if they could remove the stain, but I just couldn't imagine wearing it ever again. She asked me to at least think about it, but after a month, I decided to throw it out and pray that it never happened again. After telling this disgusting story to my supervisor, they were nice enough to excuse my lateness.

One beautiful fall morning in 2001, everyone at work was busy with their normal routines taking care of the patients and doing business as usual, and then all the TVs in our waiting areas switched over to a Breaking News report. We found out that a plane hit one of the Twin Tower buildings, and it was believed to possibly be a terrorist attack. We were all in shock because airplanes never flew that low. A few minutes later, the news reported that another building was hit by a plane. We were in shock because there was smoke and fire everywhere, and when we looked out our windows, we could see the smoke. The next thing we saw on the news was the buildings falling and people running and screaming trying to get away. I would've never guessed something like that would happen in New York. Just imagine that you woke up in the morning, dropped your kids off to school, stopped at the coffee cart for a bagel and an iced latte, and then you walked into your office, had a little chit chat with your coworkers, and five minutes later, you see an airplane headed towards your building. Imagine knowing that you are in your last minutes of life with no time to call your loved ones and say goodbye. That really taught me how short life really is.

The hospital went into lockdown; they didn't want anybody to leave. All I kept thinking about was my family. I was terrified. The cellphone lines were mostly down because those buildings probably held the towers that gave most cellphone carriers their signals. I was freaking out because I didn't like the thought of being trapped and away from my family, so I used a landline and called my house to check on everyone, making sure they were okay. I asked my sister to go get KT from school and told her that I would be home as soon as they let us out. I was considering just walking out the building, but I didn't know how I was going to get home since the trains were not running. I was contemplating walking all the way home, but there looked like thousands of people walking across bridges covered in dust and looked like they weren't going to make it. Then I was wondering if an attack was going to hit the bridges while all those people were trying to cross it, so I decided to wait it out where I felt slightly safe. I felt better knowing that my son was home, and if something happened to me, at least they were all together.

The trains began to start up slowly later on in the afternoon but had major delays and some were re-routed. Before I left work, I decided to pack a little survival kit in my bag just in case I got stuck underground on the train and couldn't get out. I filled my bag up with a bunch of healthy snacks, a few bottles of water, some alcohol pads, a few bandages, and a hospital sanitary napkin in case I had a big bloody wound that needed lots of padding. When I got on the train, it moved very slowly, and when it reached the area where the buildings fell, it moved even slower. The foundation was very unstable at that time, and the vibration of a train roaring through the tunnels underneath there would've caused more damage. We sat in the tunnel for a few minutes, and I was so afraid because I was hoping that this wasn't how life would end for me. I just sipped on my water and prayed that I wouldn't be another person buried under the rubble or never found. Once I made it to my train stop, I had a slow walk home just thinking about how grateful I was to be alive. I was still thinking about those thousands of people who went in those buildings for work and never made it out. It turned out that I did know someone who worked in one of the towers that was hit, and her remains were never found.

I was very relieved to make it home to my family. From that point forward, I started traveling with a bottle of water in my bag in case of an emergency. If I was ever trapped somewhere, I would at least have something to survive off until I was rescued. I didn't think I would ever forget seeing the pictures of people jumping out of windows to save their own lives. I'm afraid of heights, so I could never imagine that tough decision to stay in a burning building and risk not getting out somehow. That made me want to not travel back into the city for work, but unfortunately, that's where the money was.

Chapter Twelve

The issues with the trains went on for a while after the terrorist attacks, and I was constantly late for work. My job was not very understanding of this situation, and they asked me if there was any way possible for me to get to work on time. I explained to them that I couldn't drop off my son any earlier; there was literally nothing different that I could be doing. They decided to write me up, and of course, I was pissed. I had enough going on and couldn't afford any blemishes on my record because I was doing my best. I hated that I was sitting there being scolded by two women who weren't even mothers. They had no idea what I was going through, but I never asked them to care. I just hated explaining myself and telling them my personal business only for them to pass judgment on me. The whole dynamics of how the meeting was set up pissed me off too. We were in a small room, and there were three chairs in there. They asked me to sit in the chair that was lower to the ground, so that they were sitting higher, looking down on me. I took that as a form of disrespect whether it was intentional or not. I was so full of rage at that moment that I decided I was going to quit my job. I didn't have a backup plan, but at that point, I had very little control over anything else. I was holding on by a thread, and there wasn't a damn thing that I could do about it. It was pretty safe to say that my bladder and KT were all that I was controlling, and I was barely controlling my bladder.

After going back to my desk, I couldn't fix my face to disguise the anger that I felt. I was pissed, and I couldn't let it go. I was desperately trying to find a way to get my revenge, but I couldn't come up with anything. I wanted to walk off the job in the middle of the day, but I knew they would fire me. My ego wouldn't let this die down, so the next day, I decided to call out sick. I still didn't feel better, so I decided to call out sick for two more days. I knew I needed a doctor's note at that point to return to work since I missed three days, but I had no intentions on getting one. I decided to give my temp agency a call to see if they had any temp-to-permanent positions open, and they said they had some things lined up and would give me a call. That was all I needed to hear, and on my fifth day of calling out sick, I told them that I wasn't coming back. Fuck them!

I knew that quitting was the dumbest thing I could've done, but I just couldn't let them think that they could walk all over me. I felt confident enough that something else would come through fairly quickly for me. My dignity was not to be tampered with if I could help it. My God was too awesome to let me suffer for too long, and I knew that he would come through for me before I officially hit rock bottom. In the meantime, I had to go to court again to deal with the late rent payments, which I knew wouldn't work out too well, but somehow, I always made it through. About two months after that court date disaster, I got a permanent job offer to work in an orthopedic billing office in Staten Island. It was a decent paying, full-time job with good benefits and was exactly what my family needed to get us going in the right direction. Approximately two weeks before my start date, my grandpa on my father's side passed away. He lived a very long time after Nana passed. We called Grandpa "King Fish" aka "Fish" to most. He was such a cute, sweet, and peaceful old man. I couldn't understand how God could take him away, but how selfish was I to think that Nana didn't deserve to be with her husband again.

Once the day came to start my billing job, I knew I couldn't walk around feeling depressed anymore. I had to carry on with my life. It was quite a journey to get to work because I had to take the train and a ferry to get there. It was the perfect job for me because I sat at my desk all day with no phone and no distractions of a computer that gave internet access. It was an old PC that only had billing software on it. I didn't mind not talking to anybody in the office because it only turned into drama with most of the ladies. Every day, I just sat there and banged my work out. There was so much to gossip about, such as the office romance between the supervisor and two of his staff members and how at different times of the day, he would disappear with each of them.

The company had a few locations and was not doing well financially. Management began to go from site to site laying people off. I wasn't worried because I knew they usually started from the highest paid positions to the lowest when they wanted to let people go. The day before management was scheduled to come to my site, I tripped over a lose brick in the street on my way to the train station and sprained my ankle. The worst part was I had just made it through probationary period and was waiting for my insurance card in the mail. My ankle was hurting really bad and was swollen to the point where I couldn't walk on it the next day. I hated to call out sick, but I couldn't walk through the pain. Later on that day, I received a call from my supervisor telling me that I was let go from my position and to not worry about my belongings because they would mail everything to me, including my last paycheck. I guess getting laid off while you're at home is much better than having to work a whole day and then being let go. It was only six months that I was in the position, which meant that I was eligible for unemployment, so at least that would be a steady weekly check coming in. I had everybody laughing at me because it was kind of funny to get fired on your day off. Just like that, I was back on my ass looking for a way to get back on my feet. The weird part was that I wasn't really upset because I was kind of used to things not going that well for long.

That weekend, I was back on the computer fixing my resume up with all my new skills I had acquired and prepared myself mentally to start job-hunting again. For the next couple of weeks, I was just taking KT to school, sitting around talking to everybody else that didn't have a job, and making my dinner early in the afternoon. After a while, I got completely turned off from looking for a job. I was laid off in June, and I went on maybe a total of three interviews the entire summer. I did have my unemployment, so I didn't feel like a total bum. I felt more like a bum with benefits. It was like $800 a month, which wasn't too bad in 2003. The other problem was that it was the same amount as my rent. At that point, my mother was done with the babysitting game, but she still had her fixed income from the government, so she was straight. However, all the money that she had coming in always seemed to be for her to cover the expenses of the other apartment that was in her name. She had a house full of people subleasing her apartment and not one of them made sure those bills were being taken care of. Even when the

lights would get turned off, they would just get an
extension cord and plug it into the hallway to get some
light. To avoid embarrassment, my mother would always
use her money to pay the bill, and they knew she would, so
the bullshit naturally happened more than once. These were
my mother's so-called friends from when she was younger,
and she had a ridiculous soft spot for them even though
they were stumbling to the ground alcoholics and old-ass
dope fiends. Growing up in the hood teaches you not to be
judgmental because each and every one of us could say that
we know someone who was a drunk, drug addict, low-class
prostitute, low-budget pimp, teen mom, hustler, drug
dealer, or struggling working person. The worst part about
being surrounded by these things is that most people tend to
do them because they bring temporary pleasure and keep
you from having to face reality. Some people chose drugs
or liquor, but I chose men. I always made my son my first
priority though. I took him to places he saw on
commercials to give him more of a lasting memory of the
events. I even brought his little friends along sometimes
because I would feel bad that he was an only child. After I
ran him ragged by taking him here, there, and everywhere,
I would feed him good, and end the day with a bath. He
would fall asleep instantly every time, and then it was 'me'
time. The bad part was that my 'me' time didn't begin until
late at night. I had time to go for drinks, a little something
to eat, and you know the rest. After a while, I started
skipping the drinks and food and got straight to business. I
spent so much time taking care of everybody around me
that the attention of a man was what I felt like I needed. I
knew that sex didn't solve any of my problems, but it damn
sure helped me forget even if it was just for a little while. I
didn't know anybody who wouldn't trade their stress with

some forbidden pleasure for at least three to four hours out of the day.

Since I wasn't looking for love, no matter what dude came and went in my life, I would always make time and room for Mike. He was definitely my on and off again forbidden pleasure. We would go as long as a year not seeing or speaking to each other, but somehow, we would always pick up where we left off. No matter how many years went by, we could never establish a relationship. As usual, after a while, I would get frustrated with the situation and back off, and he never disputed it because he wasn't the type of guy to stress anything. I guess he knew deep down inside I would be back because I always came back. For each time that I forgave him, I realized after the fact that I was still rewarding his bad behavior by not showing him that there would be consequence of losing me if he didn't change. A man won't change if he knows he doesn't have to. I knew I had to toughen up. The problem was I didn't know where to start with my changes because I was still seeking refuge through men. I had no inner peace and no guidance on how to find it. I also didn't ask for help either. I wasn't looking for love because I had all the love that I wanted at home with my family. Unfortunately, that love came with a lot of responsibilities and stress. That was okay for me because that's all that I was used to. If life ever went well at home, I would be too afraid to celebrate. I just continued hanging out with my home girls when I could and my male friends when I felt like it. I never felt ashamed about anything I ever did because in my mind, I wasn't hurting anybody and always made sure that I was back at home before the sun came out and my son woke up.

The worst thing about hanging out late was making sure that the sun never caught me out in the streets. Words can't explain how stupid I felt doing the walk of shame to the building and seeing my neighbors who went to early morning church service. My hair was never exactly the way it looked from the night before, and I was a little too dressed up to look like I just came from the corner store. All through my twenties, this was how I coped with everyday life. My days consisted of stressing over my mother being sick, being a positive role model for my little sister, being the best mother I could be to my son, trying to earn a steady living, and fighting to keep a roof over our heads. I savored the moment to hit the streets and do a little wrong, and every now and then, I would drag a friend or two out with me so they could forget their troubles for a little while too. My friends and I would have a blast together like we didn't have a care in the world. There was no social media back then, no pictures being taken from a cellphone, and nobody trying to ruin anybody's home life, and there was plenty to ruin at that time. We all had a mutual understanding amongst each other. Nobody wanted to get married, steal anybody away, or have a baby, so it was a win-win for everybody.

Chapter Thirteen

Back in the days, married men wanted side relationships that were equal or better than what they had at home. It's really sad, but it makes for a lot of entertaining bullcrap on talk shows and Reality TV. Everybody's too busy sexing everybody, but nobody loves anymore. I felt like I already found the love of my life, and that was my son. One day, I knew I would have to get out there and search for love, and if everything went right, I hoped to be married by the time I turned 40.

After being home for a few months and going on very few interviews, I decided to go to my management office to explain to them what my financial situation was and request a smaller apartment so I could afford to pay my rent. They told me that I had to get on the waiting list for a two-bedroom. The only problem with that was that the waiting list was ten years. I couldn't understand why the hell they thought that was an option. I explained to them that ten years was unacceptable, and they told me that I should go to court and let a judge decide. Great! I had to go back to the one place I hated in the entire world. I didn't have time to spare, so I prepared myself to go down there the very next day. I had a numb feeling the very moment I stepped into the courthouse. I should've applied for a job there since I was there so much. As I entered the courtroom, I felt fearless and ready for whatever was headed my way. As I stood before the judge for the umpteenth time and explained my financial situation and the need for a smaller apartment, the judge asked me if I applied for something smaller.

"Yes, but the waiting list is ten years."

"Okay."

"In the meantime, I can't afford my apartment, so the only thing left for me to do is move."

"Okay," he said again, giving me a blank stare.

I was in shock. That fat bastard was just looking at me like he could give two shits about what I was talking about.

"I guess I have no choice but to move."

"Okay," he said for the final time, and just like that, the case was dismissed. I was so confused at how the place you are supposed to turn to for a resolution never offered one.

I walked out of that courtroom and promised myself to never return again. I knew my family would be upset to hear that we had to move, but in the end, it's what needed to happen. I knew my son would be hurt the most because he grew up in that neighborhood and all his friends were there, but that nightmare had to end. It was definitely not the type of battle I wanted to spend the rest of my life fighting.

I decided to ride the local train home so I could prepare myself on how to break the news to everyone. As soon as I walked through the door, I told my mother that it was over and that the judge couldn't help us. The bottom line was that we had to move. My son and sister were upset, and my mother was pissed off. She was determined to find a way to stay. She called everybody including her momma to try and raise money to stay, but in the meantime, the rest of us were packing up our stuff. She spent days dwelling on the situation. Once she realized that there was nobody left to help us, she let it go. She never wanted to go back to her apartment to live. She was totally content with subleasing it to a bunch of childhood friends who barely kept jobs and never paid rent. It was never to her benefit helping these people out, but that was my momma. She loved to help people even if they didn't deserve it, but the time had come for them to go. Of course, they were devastated. They didn't have anywhere to go either, but that was no longer our problem. They procrastinated on leaving, and Mommy procrastinated packing her stuff. I spent weeks sorting through our stuff and trying to figure out what to throw out and what to keep. A few weeks of preparing went by, and my mother wasn't acting like herself. She would come home from dialysis and be unusually tired. We didn't bother her at night and always let her get plenty of rest. After a few days went by, she was getting up less and less, so I started watching her closely. When she started ignoring her phone ringing and telling people she would call them back, I definitely knew there was a problem. She became severely fatigued and almost non-responsive, so I convinced her to go to the Emergency Room. To our surprise, she had walking pneumonia. I was so glad that she went in because she probably would've died in the house. While she spent a few days in the hospital, we were still at home packing up our stuff. I told her to focus on getting better, and we would take care of the rest. Since I wasn't working, I had more than enough time to sort through her stuff and pack what I thought she should keep and throw out the rest. We found some neighborhood guys with a van to move our stuff for a very affordable hood rate.

Right before our move-out date came, she was discharged from the hospital and felt much better. Our goal was to move before we owed another month's rent. The crazy part was while we were moving our stuff into the other apartment the people living there were still slowly moving their stuff out. I didn't want to go over there until they were totally gone. I couldn't stand the sight of most of them because they were just sad. I'm sure most of them grew up with a pretty decent life and even both parents at home, yet they all turned out to be drunks and drug addicts. Lord only knows what happened in their lives to make them turn to addictions, but I prayed that they all would get clean and sober one day, so they could live better lives.

I knew that I had a lot of work to do as far as the clean up once they left. I can't even bring myself to discuss the smell that came out of that house. It was one of the worst odors that I've ever smelled in my life. The only way to describe it is to imagine the mixed smell of bums and corn chips. Taking a bath or shower wasn't an option in that house. I knew that for a fact because the bathtub was loaded with junk. Cleaning the bathroom was going to be a special project for me, but until it got cleaned my way, I wouldn't be able to stay there. KT and I stayed at my bestie's house in the meantime. I planned on switching his school so he could be closer to his new home. He would have to travel on the bus eventually, and I figured that it would be a great time to teach him since he was in middle school. My sister did her best to clean the bathroom, but I still felt like it wasn't right. It was usable, but I would at least need a pair of water shoes on before I stepped foot inside the shower. I think I would've died if my skin touched any part of it. Since everybody thought I was being ridiculous, I just stayed at my friend's house a little longer until I was ready for the big cleanup day.

One day, I decided that it was a great day to clean the bathroom. I opened up all the windows, put my gloves on, and decided to do the tiles in the tub first. I threw bleach on the walls and watched the dirt slide down. It was the biggest mudslide that I've ever seen. Before my very eyes, I watched the walls go from grey to white. The smell of bleach was so strong in the house that my eyes were burning and my mother was choking and coughing really badly. I apologized, but the job had to be done. When the mission was complete, we were all in shock to see how clean the bathroom looked. It was like staring at a newborn baby for the first time. Naturally, I had to do the honors of taking the first shower. That made it official for me to spend the night and not have to leave early in the morning to go bathe.

It wasn't easy trying to adjust to the small living space, but we had to work it out. We went from a big three-bedroom to a small two-bedroom. We used to have plenty of closet space, but now, we were pretty much living out of big blue bins and bags. I put all KT's stuff in the closet so he would be properly prepared for school. Since I wasn't working, I really didn't care where most of my clothes were; I had more than enough time to organize my bins.

School was going well for KT, but he had to ride the bus there. He knew how to cross the street without a problem, but I was terrified for him to ride the bus alone. He knew the bus route and where to get off, but I was just too terrified, so I was planning on switching his school to the one right across the street from Mommy's house. I knew it was hard for kids to adjust to new schools, so I decided to let him finish out his 5th grade year in his school so he could graduate with his friends from P.S. 159. Even though we all lived there, I never called it home. It never looked or felt like home. There was always a negative vibe when I stepped foot in that house. My cellphone even had bad reception in there.

Chapter Fourteen

From childhood, I never liked the neighborhood. All my memories consisted of my mother taking me to her friends' houses for their ladies' nights. I always had to go in the room and play with their kids, and the mothers would be in the kitchen drinking rum or vodka. They would spend hours laughing and talking about their "no-good-ass" men who weren't shit, but they stayed with them anyway. I would always ditch the kids and go sit in the living room so I could be close enough to the kitchen to listen to their stories. I didn't give a damn about playing with the kids because I needed to hear all about the no-good men with the good-ass sex. I recall my last time rolling with Mommy to a ladies' night adventure. We were there until the sun came up. Strike 1 was that I never went to sleep because I could never fall asleep unless I was at home. Strike 2 was her friend's son was in his room sleep butt naked and shitted on himself and had flies flying all around him. That incident right there was enough for me to not wait on a strike 3. After that, I started hanging with my grandmother. The only bad part about that was I had to get up early on Saturday mornings to go to the city to shop in all the high-end stores. The key to shopping with Grandma was to not be annoying and sit on the mannequin stands and be quiet. I could do that without a problem so she would buy me something and treat me to lunch somewhere really nice. Those were the good 'ol days.

I knew we had to make the best of this situation, and I had to believe deep down in my heart that it would only be temporary. Here I was a grown woman sharing a room with my son and sister. I was sharing a bed with KT who was of course a wild sleeper to make matters even worse. When it was time to use the bathroom, we had to be real strategic because we didn't have a choice but to go one at a time. I spent thirty years in an apartment with two bathrooms, so this was a lifestyle shock for me. I remembered once when nature got the best of my sister, she went and pissed in the garbage. We were experiencing the true definition of 'sardines in a can'. We did have the luxury of having a TV in every room, but it was more cost effective to just watch one. We never paid for electricity in our old apartment, and now, we had to remember to cut the lights off when we walked out of rooms and unplug stuff from sockets that were not in regular use. That was quite an adjustment and something we had previously taken for granted. We went from living in a castle to living in a shoe. Thank goodness, we had really nice neighbors. They were people we had known for years and got along very well with. That helped out a great deal.

KT and I traveled back and forth to the old neighborhood every now and then to keep some sanity and to allow him the opportunity to see his old friends. I was still looking for a job, but the callbacks were coming in slowly. I was still getting unemployment checks, so I wasn't totally without funds. I went on maybe two interviews a month, so I decided to go back to my roots and started temping again. All the agencies I dealt with had lots of medical affiliations, and with my background, the calls were still coming in slow. It started stressing me out, so as usual, I dealt with my stress the only way I knew how, which was with my male friends. I knew that wasn't the answer, but it had been my answer for so many years.

The day before Halloween, I got a call from an agency to come in to register with them so they could place me on a temp-to-permanent position they thought I would be great for at the Hospital for Specialty Surgery. I went in to fill out an application, and they set me up to start the job the beginning of that next week. Six months into the assignment, they hired me permanently. This made me feel like I could have some normalcy in my life and focus on finding an apartment for me and KT. I wanted to start looking for a two-bedroom that was close to trains, so it would be easy for me to get back and forth to work, and he could travel to school. That would be the perfect opportunity for him to learn how to take the train and see the many different ways to get home in case of an emergency. High school was right around the corner, so I figured that this would be the best time for him to learn.

Apartment hunting was very difficult to do after work. I had to meet with realtors and landlords by a certain time to only end up being shown apartments that were either too small or too expensive. Plus, I had to make sure I was home at a decent time to cook dinner and help KT with his homework. Life was starting to get stressful all over again. I should've known that it wasn't quite my time to be happy just yet. Mommy was struggling with her dialysis treatments, and it was starting to break her down. She was nowhere near the top of the transplant list, and I was told that I couldn't be a donor for her because I was still at childbearing age. There was so much going on that I never found out if that was true or not. Mommy and I spoke about me being a donor, but she kept saying no. She brought me into this world, so I figured the least I could do was help her stay in it. As we all tried to move forward and be productive in our lives, I kept apartment hunting, Mommy was still going to dialysis three times a week, Jazz was in college, and KT was playing football. Things seemed like they were getting a little better and more promising, so I got more aggressive with my search and decided to look into other cities that weren't too far from what I had known my whole life. I found out that moving further away would give me the chance to live in a nicer neighborhood, which would cost me more rent and definitely a bigger deposit to move into. I didn't have enough money saved up, and I wouldn't dare consider borrowing money from anybody, so I decided to use my income tax money to take care of the situation.

One evening, Mommy started complaining about a pain in her side that she had been feeling for quite some time. The only reason why she decided to mention it was because it became unbearable. By that time, she had already lost full kidney function, so she was very worried that something might've been wrong with her liver. I wanted her to go to another hospital so she could get a second opinion, but she insisted on staying with the local hospital because it was convenient. I would never leave my health in the hands of a doctor because it was close to home, but there was no changing her mind. All I could do was have her back with the decisions that she made for herself. I pretty much spent most days with zero energy. Between Mommy going back and forth to the Emergency Room for the pain in her side, work, and football practice, I had no time for me again. I was able to take off a day from work to go with her to the doctor to hear what the plan was to figure out what was wrong with her side. The doctor said he wanted to do a liver biopsy for diagnostic testing. She agreed, but he told her that the operating room schedule was booked for months. He said he could do it faster if she came in through the Emergency Room; he could admit her that way. I didn't like the plan, but she was all for it, so there was nothing that I could do. When we left the office, we stood outside the hospital and waited for her transportation to arrive so she could go to dialysis.

"Do you think I should go through with it?" she asked, while we stood there.

"No."

"I'm not sure either," she said shrugging her shoulders, "but I don't want to wait anymore."

We stood in total silence as we both contemplated her decision to go forward with the plan or not.

Since we were approaching Thanksgiving, she told the doctor that she would do the procedure the week after that. We decided to leave the topic alone for a while and focus on having a lovely Thanksgiving because she loved the holidays. I told her that she could relax that day and let me do all the cooking; that way, she could rest. That was my first time making everything by myself. I didn't invite anybody over, but for some reason, I couldn't stop cooking. I sat the entire night at the dining room table as a rest spot while I cooked. I dozed off a few times, but I would pop back up as soon as I felt my neck jerk too hard. When daylight came, I was still up going back and forth between the pies and basting the turkey. As soon as 8 a.m. hit, I was on my way to the supermarket to get more stuff. I don't know what came over me, but I wasn't done in the kitchen until noon. When I turned that stove and oven off, suddenly, my body just shut down. I couldn't care less about food or company coming over. I fell asleep across the foot of the bed fully dressed. When I woke up, it was evening, and the house was packed with company for my mother. They were dogging the food and leaving with lots of doggy bags. I hated that, but I didn't say anything because Mommy was happy and having a good time. My grandma told me that she said that I outdid myself in the kitchen and to mark Thanksgiving 2004 as one of the best she ever had.

Chapter Fifteen

Once the holiday was over, the day came for her to go the Emergency Room so she could be admitted for the surgery. She spent one night in there before she was given a bed. They scheduled her for surgery the following day. I had to work, but me being there wouldn't stop any decisions that she wanted to make for her care anyway. She'd been in and out of the hospital so many times that I would never have imagined that stay would be more dramatic than any other time. My plan was to go up there straight from work and pray that I didn't have to see or hear about something that would piss me off and get somebody fired. I spoke to her the day before the surgery, and she said nothing was going on and to go straight home and just come after the procedure. We spoke one more time that evening, and she told me that she had to drink like a gallon of liquids the day before the procedure. I was very confused on why a renal patient would be loaded up with liquids when she had fluid restrictions on a daily basis. I was also confused on why she agreed to it. The next morning, I went to work with the full intention on going straight to the hospital after I got off. As soon as I got there, I saw that everything was going wrong. They didn't give her dialysis before the surgery, so she had a very high fluid buildup. She had complications from the anesthesia, so the procedure was never performed. They had to send her to the recovery room and prepped her to go to ICU. None of that was supposed to happen. I let her take control of her own life, and all types of mistakes happened. I was very mad at myself that I didn't fight her more to make some of the decisions. I guess I was mentally spreading myself too thin, but I had to be there for her. Every day, there was always an incident at the hospital that was telling me that I had to get her out of that place. The biggest issue was catching her doctors during the day. One was always missing in action during the day, and the other one at night never had the right answers to my questions. Mommy was having a very slow recovery, and nothing was adding up. She spent Christmas and New Years in the hospital, and my frustration was building up because she never spent the holidays away from home.

Once she was transferred to a regular room, I felt a slight relief. She was on her regular dialysis schedule, but she still didn't feel better. She never recovered enough to be rescheduled for her biopsy. I was having a hard time focusing at work because I was trying to make calls to reach social workers, administrators, and doctors, but someone was always giving me the run around. I wrote a few complaint letters that got me responses like, *We're doing our best to give your mother the best care possible.* At that point, her spirits were low, and she wasn't acting much like herself. The one time that I thought she was on her way back to normal was when she told me she was tired of hospital food and asked me to make her some lima beans with white rice and ham. The next day, I showed up with exactly what she asked for. She loved the food but said that I made too much. I wasn't worried about that because I knew her so-called boyfriend would more than likely eat the rest. He was always around to take whatever she had.

At that point, she had been in the hospital for over a month and a half with no discharge date in sight. I had enough, so I prepared to take over. She was getting very agitated and would call me at two and three in the morning complaining that she was trying to reach the nurses' station, but they wouldn't answer the call bell. She would be yelling at me to do something. I couldn't go up to the hospital floors that time of night, so I would stay up calling the nurses' station to tell them to go to her room. Then I would call her back to make sure they came. I would battle to go back to sleep for another hour or so before it was time for me to get up for work. That went on for like two weeks straight, and I was so frustrated that I would be crying once I got off the phone with her. She would always put pressure on me to fix things, and like a fool, I would try, knowing that I couldn't.

One evening, I came to visit her late because I went to get my taxes done. When I told her where I was, she didn't seem interested. Money was always important to her, and now, she didn't care and she was starting to lose her appetite. This had me worried because she was losing her desire for everything that she cared so much about. I decided to put in for a weeklong vacation, so I could work on getting her transferred out of that hospital. On the 19th, they received a call from another institution, discussing her transfer. Suddenly, everybody from doctors to social workers wanted to talk to me, but it was too late. I told my mother that I was getting her out of there. She was so depressed and kept saying that they didn't know what they were doing and that she was going to die there. I kept telling her to stop saying that but she wouldn't. I spent the whole afternoon until visiting hours were over just sitting there with her. We were both quiet, but just being in each other's presence was good enough. She took a long nap, and I took one too. Around 7 p.m., I told her that I had to go so I could catch the supermarket and buy something quick to cook.

"I'll be back first thing in the morning to get the transfer started."

"Okay," she said, but her face had disappointment written all over it. She always knew how to make me feel guilty about doing what I knew was right.

While I was waiting for the elevator, her so-called man was in the waiting area. I guess he was there so he could be alone with her to steal her money or eat her food. I just looked at him and gave a half-ass hello before I left. It started snowing, so I had to slip and slide my way to the supermarket real fast before they closed. I picked up something quick to cook for KT, and after he was done eating, I sent him to bed. Then I went to my friend's house where all my work stuff was and planned on sleeping there for the night. KT was home with my sister and her boyfriend, so I didn't have to worry.

Chapter Sixteen

A round 12:30 a.m., I received a call from the hospital telling me that my mother had taking a turn for the worse and I should come up there. I never got a call like that before, so I didn't know what to expect. I guessed that she was unconscious or something and they needed to make a medical decision that I had to sign paperwork for. When I got there, security let me go right upstairs. When I got to her floor, the nurses' station was quiet, and they asked me to sit in the office to speak with the doctor.

A few minutes later, a nurse came in the room. "How you feeling?" she asked.

"I'm okay," I said, but I knew something was wrong.

The doctor came in with a very soft-spoken tone and said, "As we were doing our rounds, your mother was found unconscious. We tried many times to revive her, but we couldn't."

I just looked at her and asked, "Is she dead?"

"Yes...I'm very sorry. The time of death was 12:12 a.m."

I felt completely lost. I was supposed to be transferring her the next day, so why was she dead? I went to her room to see her. She was wrapped up in a sheet, but her face was out. I lifted the sheet and saw a tag on her toe. I think I stood there for thirty-minutes crying. After getting some control, I picked her bag up and left. The only thing that I could do was think about why I was going through that all alone. Then I remembered that booty calls were not there for you emotionally and didn't give any moral support.

I stood in the lobby of the hospital to call a cab so I could go tell my sister and son the news. The hardest part was calling my grandparents and breaking the news to them. I played that moment out a million times in my head, and yet I was still unprepared. The call was very brief, and they handled it better than I thought. I always believed older people tend to accept death as just a part of the life cycle, or maybe, they were just being strong for me.

As I approached the door to our house, I stood there for a minute because I just didn't know how to word this. For some reason, I didn't use my key, but instead, I rang the doorbell. It was 1:30 a.m., so I'm sure I startled my sister. When she opened the door and saw me with Mommy's bag in my hand, she already knew what happened. Her heart looked like it stopped for a minute. She ran in the room and fell apart.

"I'm so sorry, but there was nothing they could do."

KT was sleeping, and I just couldn't tell him that his grandma was gone. My bestie came over with her hair wet in a plastic cap to sit with me. We sat at the dining room table until the sun came up and barely said two words to each other. If I didn't consider her family before, I knew it then. Once the sun rose, she hugged me and left to go home. I waited until it was time for KT to get up for school then I explained to him that she got really sick, and the doctors tried to help her, but she didn't make it.

"Did she die?" he asked with one tear rolling down his face.

I shook my head and said, "Yes."

He cried so bad that all I could do was say I was sorry. He even stepped up like a big boy and rang one of my neighbor's bell to tell them the news. I was so confused on what I should've been doing over the next couple of days. I didn't want to be okay. I didn't want to talk to people. I wanted and needed it to be a bad dream. I wanted to sit on the floor and cry for days, but instead, I fought my feelings and stayed busy, holding my tears in until I was alone. The only emotion that I ever felt comfortable displaying was anger. I always felt that showing my sensitive side would make people want to take advantage of me.

I kept myself busy until my grandparents arrived to town. I started cleaning the apartment out, throwing away things that were just taking up space. Then I had to go up to the hospital to see an administrator and sign some documents. The same nurse who wouldn't help me decided to show up to the office to give me a sympathy talk. If my mouth wasn't so dry, I think I would've spit right in her face. After I left the hospital, I went with my grandparents to the funeral home. I was learning how to make final arrangements, and the only time I spoke was to help pick out the casket. That was another moment where I wanted to lose it, but I stayed strong because I didn't know the feelings my grandparents had having to bury their child.

The next day, Jazz and I went to my mother's favorite dress store to buy her something new to be laid to rest in. Her favorite colors were white and cream, so we had a bunch of two-piece outfits to choose from. The sales lady was really nice and helpful. As soon as she asked us what the occasion was, I almost lost it. All I could do was shake my head and walk away. I couldn't believe we were buying the last outfit that she would ever wear again. I went and stood by the front door and waited for my sister to bring the outfit to the register. I didn't mean to leave her hanging like that, but it was just too much for me to handle.

When we got home, I prepped her bag with the outfit, earrings, stockings, undergarments, and a wig. My mother was very much into getting her hair done, and I knew the funeral parlor would never be able to do her hair to her liking. As I entered the funeral parlor, I felt her presence. I could almost hear her asking me to come get her out of there because she wasn't supposed to be there. I rushed out so I wouldn't start crying, but of course, I couldn't help myself. Once again, I had another moment alone wishing I had somebody, just anybody, by my side to hug me or hold my hand. It was freezing outside with snow and ice on the ground, and I was trying to figure out where were those guys who knew my number when they were lonely but nowhere around when I needed a hug.

The night before the wake, I couldn't sleep. I felt like something was wrong. Even after death, my mother still had the power to make me feel guilty. I felt like she wasn't satisfied with her final appearance. I had the weirdest feeling that they cut her hair when they took her bun out so they could put her wig on. It was almost like I could hear her cursing and carrying on not to touch her hair. I cried myself to sleep and was loaded with guilt that her hair wasn't like she wanted it. When I woke up that morning, I was such a wreck on the inside. For the first time in months, I really took a good look at myself. My face didn't look older, but it looked tired and worn out. As I parted my hair down the middle, it was very thin and brittle. I was a hot mess and didn't even realize it. I asked the Lord to get me through the situation first, and then I would start getting myself together.

Chapter Seventeen

My sister and grandparents went to the wake early to make sure Mommy looked okay before our friends and family were due to arrive. KT and I showed up a little later because I wanted to make sure he was mentally prepared to see his grandmother laying in a casket. As we entered the funeral home, we smiled and said hello to those standing outside of the room. The closer we got to the door, the more I felt like I was going to throw up. I fought the feeling hard by smiling and hugging everyone. After a while, I felt like I was in the twilight zone. I felt like I was looking through the face of everyone there. As I stood with KT taking my last look at my mother, for some reason, I still felt like she was unhappy. It's funny to me that living people can say that dead people are in a better place as if they've died before, taken a tour of heaven, and then came back to life to let everybody know how it looks. She was too full of life to be okay with being dead at the age of 48.

I ran my hand up her arm, and it was cold. That made me cry even more because I wanted to put a blanket over her to help her get warm.

"I'm sorry, Mommy," I whispered, "I hope you know that I tried my best to help. I'm just sorry that my best wasn't good enough."

KT was occupied by some of his friends, so I was glad for that, but when it was time to leave, reality set in. He screamed and cried so bad that I almost couldn't pull him away from the casket. One of her drunk friends was there trying to make him laugh as a distraction, but I had to yell at him to just go and let me deal with him. I ended up just standing there and hugging him while he got the screams out. Once he calmed down, we slowly walked out. I don't think I ever had a headache like the one I had that night. Going to sleep was the only thing I could do to take that pain away.

We got up early the next morning to prepare for the funeral. We all did pretty well at the service until we had to watch my grandparents say goodbye to their child. That turned everybody into an emotional wreck. As we cruised along the highway to the cemetery, I was busy thinking about everything that went wrong at the hospital and if I really did enough. My brain could never get a rest I swear. While we stood around her casket listening to the preacher pray over us, I asked the funeral director where would she be buried, and he pointed at the exact spot. It was a few feet away with a big pile of snow sitting there. I wasn't okay with leaving her in the cold while they cleaned her spot out. He explained to me that they didn't lower caskets in front of the family there. Grandma sat in the car because I guess she couldn't take anymore, and there was snow and ice on the ground, which was dangerous for her at her age. Everyone said goodbye and walked back to their cars. My sister and I were the last to walk away. She hovered over the casket like she was giving Mommy a big hug. I ran my hands across the head of the casket and said goodbye, and I could've sworn that I heard her say goodbye to me in a very disappointing tone. It was that tone that you use right before you're about to cry. I knew she was pissed and didn't want to be out there because she spent her whole life in New York, and now, her final resting place was in New Jersey.

I spent three weeks home from work because I just didn't feel like talking about her death. I needed normalcy in my life. I didn't want a pity party either. I just wanted to be able to have regular conversations and make it through the day without having a breakdown. I had to be strong for my family at all times. If I got stressed out, then they might get stressed out too. We were all we had and had to be strong so our grandparents wouldn't have to worry about us. With that time off, I spent most of my days going through her belongings and giving stuff away. I also threw stuff out that she would never have considered to be trash.

I was so in control of my emotions that I would plan when I would let out a good cry. I would actually hold it in until everybody was asleep or while I took a shower. If I was having a really bad day and had an urge to cry, I would just save it for a day when nobody was home and scream at the top of my lungs, letting the tears fall until I fell asleep.

Once I went back to work, I felt pretty good. I felt like I could make it through a whole workday without getting upset. I had a strict policy in place where I did not allow anyone to ask me questions about my mother. I only spoke about her when I felt like I could handle it without being too emotional. I spent most of my days quiet and reflecting on life. I would just think about the fact that my mother left this earth before she was 50, and I had to make sure that the same thing didn't happen to me. I started exercising in the house during my free time. I even cut down on my carbs. One night, I was doing a kickboxing workout and was so hyped that I hit my knee during the sets super hard and hurt it. The pain was so intense that I had to go see a doctor. I found out that my kneecap was loose. That explained why I was so clumsy for years. Sometimes, I would be walking and just randomly lose balance and fall. For many years, my mother thought that I needed my head examined. She was sure that I had a brain disorder because nothing else could make me that clumsy. Unfortunately, the best way to solve that problem was to have surgery to tighten the ligaments back up behind my kneecap. That would prevent my knee from dislocating again. The crazy part about it all was I probably wouldn't have had that issue at 30 if I would've had my knee looked at when I injured it at 15.

I really couldn't afford to be out of work for surgery, but I couldn't stand to walk around in pain any longer either, so I booked the surgery. I made sure I did as much grocery shopping as I could before my big day and got all my laundry done. I also made sure all my bills were paid up-to-date. The only problem that I had was trying to figure out how I was getting home from the hospital. My friend Tricey said she would take a taxi with me and help me get home. As usual, there were no guys around to help me through my time of need. My recovery from the surgery was very long and draining. I used up all my sick time and vacation time, so I could keep money coming into the house. The best part about being home was actually the painkillers. I swear oxy had to be the best invention since sweet potato pie. My prescription said to take two pills every six hours. I followed these instructions immediately after surgery, and I never felt any pain during my recovery. I also noticed that after taking the pills, at least twenty minutes later, I would fall asleep. After two weeks, my ritual was to take the pills and go lay down and patiently wait to fall asleep. As my bottle started getting empty, I began to panic. The thought of running out of pills terrified me. I called my doctor ASAP for a refill. His office even helped me get it delivered from my local pharmacy. When the delivery guy showed up, he thought he was picking up a prescription and not dropping one off. I was so mad that I almost dropped my crutches to grab his ass up and kill him. He was very apologetic and promised to come right back with my pills. When I closed the door, Jazz was looking at me in shock. She told me at that moment that I was addicted to the oxy. I denied it to her face, but deep down, I knew she was right, but I couldn't help it. They made me feel so good. I never wanted to feel any pain ever again. I didn't have a care in the world when I was taking them. At that moment, I had a better understanding of the struggles that many people have that suffered from pill popping. After spending two months home from work and doing nothing but rehab and medicating myself heavily for nothing, I realized that it was time to go back to work. I used up all my PTO and my bills were getting backed up. My only fear was going back to work and not being able to go up and down the stairs in the train station. The last thing that I wanted to do was fall down a flight of stairs. Those were the times when I wished that I had a husband to hold me down and take care of the house while I took my time getting better. Where were all the men I knew who were free late at night when I needed my light bill paid or some food in my fridge? The answer was they were not there for that, and I didn't set my standards to a level where they knew that they had to be there for me. I also didn't make sure that I had a savings account set up for emergency purposes. The bottom line was that I had to get my shit together. The crazy thing was that I was used to struggling, and I didn't know any other way in this world. I knew it was time to try though.

Chapter Eighteen

I had a really hard time commuting because I was still limping, but I knew that it would only be temporary. I was also slowly weaning my way off dealing with men who were really never there for me. They never mistreated me, but they also never wanted much from me. I accepted full responsibility for the situations I was in. I was only getting what I asked for. I was a grown woman who had to start believing and wanting more for herself. I knew there were some things in life that I couldn't change because they were God's will, but one thing I was sure of was that God would never bless me with my own man if I kept dealing with somebody else's.

Moving forward with a clean conscience was different, but it felt good. My family and I spent lots of time just learning to adjust to being home without Mommy. Mike and I started talking again and spending a little bit of time together. He was still a sweetheart. I knew he still wasn't ready to give me the type of relationship that I deserved, but I still put the effort into trying to spend more time with him and to talk with him as much as possible. I didn't get the feeling that he had another woman, but whenever I went to his house, I looked for evidence of other women being around. I knew him for years and felt that I deserved to know if there was somebody else. If I did find out about somebody else, then that would explain why our relationship never went to the next level. He had hair so having a comb wasn't suspicious, and he kept lots of good smelling body washes, so that wasn't proof of another woman either. Then one day, I spent the night at his house and left for work from there. He left for work before me and as I was getting ready, I noticed a silk scarf underneath his bed. I had the biggest bitch fit ever and went crazy in his house. I was screaming and hollering. I'm sure the neighbors heard me, but I didn't care. I started throwing change from his change bucket around the room and ripped the scarf into pieces. That made me feel better.

After I got to work, I called him and went off on him, but since he wasn't the type to argue and go back and forth, he just basically said "whatever" and hung up the phone. After I calmed down a little, I tried to talk to him, but he wanted no parts of my crazy-ass at that point. I had to let him be. I figured if we were meant to be or at least speak again then so be it, but I knew that the relationship was dead.

Our first Thanksgiving without Mommy was approaching, and it was a little awkward to think about because she loved the holidays. I knew we couldn't break the tradition, so I planned to cook again. The only problem with cooking for that day was that I always ended up cooking too much. When I was done preparing the food, we all stood in front of the spread and couldn't even begin to figure out how we were going to eat it all. We had to make the most of the day, but there was definitely a void that couldn't be filled. We were missing the presence of Mommy. We didn't have any visitors like we expected. All the people who promised to be there for us and to keep in touch were gone. That taught me that people will say anything that sounds good to grieving people.

Christmas was quiet for us as well, but we made the best of it. Over the next couple of years, I spent quite some time struggling financially due to being sued by creditors and them seeking their money through garnishments. I wasn't living above my means, but I at least had to leave room in my budget to get my hair and nails done, and clothes shopping seemed to only be for KT because it always felt wrong to do things for myself. I never put my wants or needs first. One day, I would learn to take care of me. The time finally came for KT to graduate from the 8th grade at Ella Baker Middle School on the upper east side of the city. That was a very big moment in his life because high school would be the start of him attending a really large school. Most high schools in the city were over crowded. I just prayed that he wouldn't get distracted by all that was going on there.

He went to his first little junior high prom, which was during the day, so I wasn't worried about that. He and his friends had expensive tastes, and I couldn't have him looking like we were doing bad, so I went way over budget buying him expensive shoes to go with his linen outfit and a fresh pair of sneakers to go with his graduation outfit. There was plenty of food, snacks, juice, and soda at the prom, but of course, the kids wanted to go out to eat afterwards. That shit got on my last nerve, but I let it slide because you only graduate from junior high once.

I knew that I had to do whatever I could to make him happy that day because minutes before we left for his prom, his father called him to tell him that he wouldn't be able to make it to his graduation. I was so confused on why he would wait until the last minute to disappoint him, but then I had to remember that being a disappointment was all he knew how to be. KT was very upset right before leaving the house, but I knew he would cheer up as soon as he saw his friends. I called his father's good friend Frankie who I had known since I was a little girl, to let him know about the latest bullshit that was going on, and he showed up to the graduation to our surprise with hard bottom shoes on and all. We were so happy to see him come through for KT because he definitely didn't have to. We will always be forever grateful for that and will forever call him "Uncle Frizz".

When the time came for him to start high school, I decided to put him in private school because it seemed feasible with the help of financial aid. It was very depressing for me initially because it meant that he was growing up. On the other hand, it meant that I could start focusing on me a little more. I figured that it would the perfect time to go back to school and get my degree. I decided to choose a school near my job so I wouldn't have an issue being on time. I was so tired between the everyday stress of work and the weight of the world that I had been carrying around for years. Two months after school started for KT, the financial aid that I was hoping for didn't come through, and I had to take him out in November. I had to get him into a public school, and it was very difficult. I had to go to different district offices to find a decent school in Manhattan. He spent the entire month of December home while we were waiting for an answer on what school he would be accepted to. He was finally accepted to Murray Bergtraum High School. Since the decision didn't come until a week before Christmas, he couldn't start school until the holiday break was over in January.

Things were so bad for me mentally that I only lasted one year in school. I was tired of being tired. Those school days were also days that I could've stayed at work making overtime to keep up with my bills. I weighed my financial options and decided to drop out of college. It seemed like the more overtime I did, the more taxes came out of my check. My W-2 showed that I made more money that year than the previous year, and my tax returns were less and less every year. What kind of world are we in where you lose more money to the government because you tried to do better for yourself by making more? I'm sure that's where the idea of working off the books came into place. "They" say put your money in the bank and let it collect interest, but when the end of the year comes, your interest is only a few dollars off the thousands that they received off you for the year. That made me understand why a lot of old school people stacked their money in shoeboxes, safes, and underneath hardwood floors.

My private life didn't get any better either. I always had me a boo thang in the midst of my crazy life, but it was never serious enough to keep me out the streets. My friends and I hit the streets every now and then for a little nightlife fun. It was the same old thing when we were out just dancing, laughing, drinking, and socializing. Before you knew it, the night had taken you away from all your troubles, and then some dude had to come along and disturb your groove. They can never just come up to you and ask you to dance. They always come up on you humping you to the beat of the music. After a while, it felt like sex with your clothes on. Then he would want your phone number with the hopes of getting some tail really quick. It was the same scenario over and over again. They all just wanted sex. Since I was a little older, I couldn't just blame the men anymore. Women entertained the bullshit, so that's what we got out of the situation. For decades, women have been screaming, "men ain't shit!" Honestly, some of us women aren't shit either. The same way some guys just want sex, some of us just want sex too, or sometimes, we just do it for the money or material things. Sometimes, we choose to go out there and sacrifice our souls for a dollar. Sometimes, those few disgusting hours with a man every now and then really helped out with a few odds and ends. There have been times where I've come home and the water wouldn't be hot enough to wash away the memories of the night before. You get what you put out when it comes to life. I knew better, but it always baffles me as to why I never did better. I guess for some reason, it just always seemed easier to slack off. I was really determined to break my old ways and bad habits. There were just so many different struggles to work on. The most important factor to work on was my personal character. I spent a lot of years hearing people say that I was mean, but I didn't want to carry that label around anymore. I started to watch what I said to people and most importantly how I said it. I've learned that your delivery when speaking to a person determines how they receive your message. I also started making it a point to put people in their proper place in my life. There was a place for good friends, for associates, and then there were the people who you just knew. There had to be some space made between me and my associates. They didn't need to know all my business because they would most likely be the ones to spread my business or use it against me one day. Then there was my family and the place that I had to create for them in my life. As I got older, I noticed that I spent more time around my friends than my family. I didn't understand why, but it was probably in my best interest not to try and figure that out. It seemed like everybody went away when Mommy died and kind of forgot about us.

We are now in a world where the internet has become a major factor in our lives. That has definitely become the new way stay in touch, and so far, it's been working for me. If we don't know the answer to something, we've stopped asking people. We now look everything up on the internet. Kids in this lifetime don't know anything about dictionaries or encyclopedias. Now, with us having social media, we are learning to be more distant and anti-social. Nobody wants to talk on the phone anymore. If you want to reach out to a person, it has to be via text, email, or instant messaging. I've said some of the sweetest things through an email or text. I've also had some of the biggest arguments on the planet the same exact way. The best part about social media is being able to reconnect with friends from as far back as elementary school, high school, or even old neighbors. It has become an absolute blessing to see old faces again, and I've even made some new friends along the way too.

Chapter Nineteen

It was the spring of 2010, and life was pretty calm at the moment. The family was all into their normal daily activities, which was work and school. I had my male friends who I saw occasionally but nothing special that required commitment. I pretty much spent most evenings trolling through social media sites. This was my way of staying out of trouble and not being in a man's face. I would spend hours liking people's posts and comments and talking to my friends through instant messaging. Social media was quite exciting at that time because I was reconnecting with a lot of old friends from school. I stumbled upon a picture of one of my old friends from high school named Monty. He looked exactly how I remembered. I sent him a private message being my usual old rude self and said, "You better remember me!" I prayed that he recognized the fat version of the girl he used to know. To my surprise, he did. We became friends online, and not soon after that, we started keeping in touch quite often over the phone. We actually had long conversations that lasted half the night. After a while, I was cutting my sleep short just to talk to him. I would be so tired in the morning going to work, but I didn't care. He told me that he had a crush on me in high school but didn't do anything about it because I was mean. I didn't believe him because I'm sure he said that to a whole bunch of girls he had reconnected with. I knew that I was mean and I was used to people reminding me, so all I could do was say, "Sorry" and shake my head in annoyance. Monty was very sweet to me and was always a gentleman. He showed great interest in what my likes and dislikes were, and it felt good because for once, a man wasn't just concerned with sleeping with me. That was absolutely a breath of fresh air. We spent a lot of time catching up over the phone. He made it clear that he was in no rush to see me, and I liked that. He was very open and honest with me, and I appreciated that too. He knew that I was single, so he had no choice but to keep it real with me about his relationship status. I made it clear that I was the type of person to only believe what I saw and not what I heard. He told me that he was in a relationship that was on the rocks, and of course, I didn't believe him. There were always two sides to every story. Since we were old friends, I wasn't concerned or bothered by his personal issues with his woman because I wasn't looking for a relationship or anything else outside of conversation. I'd been through way too much to get in the middle of anybody else's mess. I was too busy trying to fix my own.

Monty was a really good friend to me and eventually a great hang out partner. He quickly earned the spot as my best male friend because he was always down to hang out and just talk. One day, I received a very irate call from him saying that he was having a big problem at home, and he wanted to know if he could move his stuff into my place for a short while. I was stunned, shocked, and scared all at the same time. I never spent more than a weekend with a man, so the thought of possibly forever scared the crap out of me. I told him that I had to get back to him because my son and sister didn't know him that well, and I had to make sure that they were comfortable first. I spoke with them, and they were okay with it because he was always nice whenever they saw him.

I knew that I had to clarify some things with him before I gave my final answer. Being that I never lived with a man before, we had to discuss what was going to happen between us because this meant that we had to be together. There was no way possible that I could live with a man as "just friends". When we had our conversation, I didn't give him an ultimatum, but I made it very clear that he couldn't stay with me unless we were going to be in a relationship. He agreed since we already liked each other, so we decided to give it a try. In the back of my mind, I was hoping that he didn't agree to my terms just because his back was against the wall.

Once he officially moved in, I kept my fingers crossed that the whole house would get along, and they did. The only problem was him and his ex still beefing. I know when people break up, there's always a lot of finger pointing, but at that point, I didn't understand why they still had anything to talk about, but for a while, I decided that I would hold my tongue. Shortly after that, we went on a friends and family outing, and while everybody went to go play volleyball, I decided to just watch before I ended up breaking my wrist. While I sat and watched everyone else play, his phone started going off with a bunch of text messages from his ex. She was clearly knee deep in her emotions because she was still bringing up the past and asking him if he was really coming back home. I fought the feeling and didn't go into his phone to read the earlier messages, but if he promised her that he was going back then we had a problem. When I confronted him about it, he said he didn't know where she got that idea from but swore that he had no intentions on going back to a place where he wasn't wanted. I know people tend to go backwards sometimes after a bad break up, so I was on high alert. Before he moved in, he said it would only be temporary, but after a few months of cohabitating, I was getting used to him being there. It was nice to wake up every morning to someone. It wasn't that difficult to add a little extra food in the pot for another plate, and the rest of the house was adjusting well, so I was pleased about that. Soon, the beefing with his ex seemed to die down a little. I didn't want to get on him for talking to her or have to choke her out for keeping my name in her mouth, but just when I started to feel comfortable with my new relationship, I got a wakeup call.

One day, he left the house computer on. While I was cooking, I decided to go online to see what the job market was looking like. As soon as I tapped the spacebar to wake up the screen, his social media page popped up. Being that this was the house computer, I felt entitled to look at whatever was in front of me. In my opinion, you should always log out of anything personal if you don't want anyone to read it. Of course, I looked at his private messages, and to my surprise, there were multiple conversations with multiple women. Some of the conversations were about them remembering the good old days and some were of a sexual nature. I honestly wasn't shocked because nothing usually shocked me when it came to men. I was used to being the woman who entertained these dumb-ass conversations with men. At that point, I knew what the women of those lying-ass men felt like when they saw my messages with their boyfriends. I had to let him know that I saw everything and didn't like it.

"Why didn't you log me out?"

"If you didn't want me to see anything, then don't leave it open for me to see."

"I'm sorry for you seeing what you saw, but I swear that there's nothing going on with those women."

I was still bothered by it because he apologized for me seeing the messages but not for writing the messages, and that's a big difference. At that point, I felt like I was in the middle of a big mess. I really cared about him though. We had lots of good times together and always laughed and joked a lot like two old friends should have. He was not only my best friend, he was my boo, and I loved him.

Chapter Twenty

The little issues we had also triggered my investigative ways. As much as I wanted to believe his excuses and apologies, I knew that old habits didn't die easily. My curiosity was at an all-time high, and I found myself curious to know if the chatting with other women had stopped. I watched him type in his passcode to his phone a million times and never cared. However, at that time, I couldn't resist the burning desire to use it myself. I fought the feeling as much as I could for weeks. Then one day, I decided to give in and check his phone. I waited until he fell asleep to snoop, and between the text messages and emails with multiple women, I was pissed. I knew what my chances were on seeing something that I didn't want to see were great and that I would only be hurting my own feelings. Some would prefer not to know, but I'm a 'need to know' type of woman.

The conversations were full of flattery and hopes of acting on sexual desires. The only thing that was funny to me was that he actually used the same line on different women, and of course, they all fell for it. Since I had no business snooping, I couldn't say anything. I got exactly what I asked for, but I needed to decide what I was going to do with the information. I decided to not do anything at first. I was actually curious to see how far these situations would go. It turned into a sickness for me. Snooping is a terrible addiction, and it can make a person go crazy if it goes on for too long. It will consume your every moment, and I took advantage of every opportunity I had to snoop whether it was when he went to the store, bathroom, washed dishes, or even slept. I couldn't control myself at all. I had to see the words he wrote and the pictures they swapped. When I saw that he started talking to his ex again and promised her another chance at love, I had to say something. I knew he would go crazy because I touched his phone, but I saw her messages in the midst of me trying to get the contact info of some of his closest friends to throw him a surprise birthday party. Instead, I got the surprise. It was very hard for me to understand why his ex wouldn't just go away. My ex did without a big struggle, so what was their situation really about? It was obvious that she wasn't keeping herself around. He was entertaining the nonsense. I never reached out to her about the bullcrap. I never wanted to be one of those women who got all angry with the next woman. I wasn't dealing with her, so if I was feeling some type of way about an issue with my relationship, I needed to step to the person I was in the relationship with. I did contemplate making a folder of all the pictures of these chicks and posting them publicly on the internet, but I guess that was just my petty side kicking in. I let the idea go, but I'm sure they would've been horrified if they knew that I saw their photos. I swear some women need to just stick to headshots and some shouldn't even send pictures out at all. There are a lot of faces in this world that only a mother could love. Geesh! I can definitely say it wasn't looks that was keeping his attention with some of these women. Maybe they were really nice women who were beautiful on the inside. I couldn't put my finger on what his type of woman was. It kind of made me hate women I didn't know because I would look at somebody and wonder if he wanted to fuck them. I wanted to kill all women so he had nobody else to look at. I used to tell him that I was going to snatch his eyes out, rip his penis off, and put it in my pocketbook while he goes outside. That way, he couldn't see no women and fuck no women. I was really losing my mind and struggled internally to get a grip. I probably should've went to counseling, but I didn't want anyone besides my friends to know that I was a lunatic.

Of course, we had an argument about the messages, but the most important part of it all to him was me touching his phone. Despite the bickering about other women, we actually made time for date nights. We were best friends after all and had good times together. With all the fighting about other women, I was starting to feel like the feelings weren't totally mutual. I knew that eventually time would tell me whatever he was feeling. Sometimes, I would actually walk around laughing and joking with him, but in the back of my mind, I wondered if there were any updates in his inbox from those heffas. We would never even argue if we didn't have to discuss those chicks. When you have a discussion with someone about making a bad decision, you always hope they get the point in the end and learn from their mistakes. He chose to entertain these women, and I could safely say that it wasn't because he was lacking anything at home. I had my role as "wifey" under control. I gave him everything he needed in my opinion, so the fact that he kept chasing tail was just out of pure greed. If there was something about me that wasn't quite right, I wasn't really sure, and he didn't tell me. I know there were times that I got on his nerves, but I don't think any of it warranted talking to other women.

For months, I didn't know why I was dealing with this, knowing that it was contributing to keeping my blood pressure elevated. I had a teenage son, so I didn't need any more stress than that. Then one day, it hit me, and I figured out why I was going through all that nonsense with him and all these women. Karma! That was it. I found my answer and solved my own puzzle. Karma finally caught up with me. All those years I spent being the other woman and being part of the reason some man was bringing misery to his own home had finally arrived and kicked me square in the ass. I must've been crazy to think that my payback would never come. It was my time to say that I knew what it felt like to not be the only one.

I wasn't legally bound or stuck in the relationship, but I felt that it was time to pay my dues. I decided not to walk away from him because that would be like running away from my payback. I was sure that nobody would understand my way of thinking, but I didn't expect anyone to. I've always been really hard on myself so that just went along with the territory. I knew it wouldn't last forever, so I chose to be a big girl and just take it. Things were not always bad, but I stayed prepared for the drama whenever it came. I knew I was jeopardizing my health and wellbeing with all that snooping crap and had to stop. I had to learn to trust that whatever was happening in the dark would eventually come to light, so I apologized to him and promised to stop snooping. I began to feel better instantly after giving up my spying career because it was an addictive sickness that always did more harm than good. Our relationship grew stronger after that, and we started getting along a lot better. I started focusing on more important things. It was finally time for us to move into a bigger apartment. We literally had nowhere to run and nowhere to hide. The only alone time we had in the house was on the toilet.

I constantly went all around Brooklyn viewing two-bedrooms. Everything that I did like required excellent credit. Of course, I had poor credit, so instead of the realtor charging me one to two months of security, they wanted to charge me four months. I figured if I could give someone that then I might as well have saved up for a down payment on a house, but with poor credit, a house wasn't an option either. So, I stepped out on a leap of faith and decided to look in New Jersey. I knew it could work as long as I had an easy way to get back to work in New York. The rent was cheaper and required less money down, so it was a winning situation. Jazz decided that she didn't want to stay in the apartment and moved out on her own. I was hoping that she kept Mommy's apartment since her name was already on the lease, but she was ready to step out and make her own way in this world, so I had to respect that. She was a tough girl, so I knew that I didn't have to worry about her. KT finished high school, so there was no reason for us to stay either.

After going to visit a very large two-bedroom apartment, I had to apply immediately and get my credit checked. The apartment had hardwood floors, a dining area, and the ultimate bonus was the closet space. I knew I had to live there and didn't plan on looking at any other places. I had found the one. In two days, I received an acceptance call, and I was completely shocked and terrified at the same time. Nothing usually went my way, so it felt like a prank. I was waiting for the manager to laugh and say, "Sike! Now, girl, you know damn well your credit ain't getting your ass no apartment." Instead, she congratulated me and asked me to pick a move-in date.

"Is two weeks quick enough?"

"That's a little soon," I told her because I didn't have a dime saved, "Do you think we can make it a month?"

"Of course!"

I didn't know if I would have all the money that I needed by then, but I was going to try. If it was meant to be, then it would happen. Every now and then, I would call up to heaven and ask my mother if she could ask God to do me a favor. When the heavens above teamed up to take care of me, it was amazing how everything always fell right into place. I knew that I had to make great sacrifices to make sure I had all my money for this apartment. For the next five weeks, I barely ate or drank anything. There was no room in my budget for food. I had to cancel Christmas as well. My baby wasn't a baby anymore, so he understood. Even if he didn't, that was too damn bad because a brand-new place to live was way better than any gift that I could ever give him besides the gift of life.

The move couldn't have come at a better time because we had all reached our limits from being in that little apartment. There were never a lot of happy memories in that place to begin with. No matter where I walked in there, I would get a flashback of something bad. I didn't believe there was any furniture or decorations that I could've added to make it feel like a home. The entire time that I spent in there was filled with depression, lost hope, anger, and resentment. I think I was the only person at work who was never in a rush to go home. The move to our new place was going to be my rebirth.

Chapter Twenty-One

KT was approaching the last leg of his teenage years and seemed to be losing his way in the world. He used to be so goal-oriented, and then all of a sudden, he could give two shits about anything. I know kids have a mind of their own, and no matter what you try to instill in them, they will still do what they want to do in the end. No matter how hard I tried to not blame myself, it didn't work. I tried to manage my time right and divide it equally amongst everything and everyone who was important, but I just couldn't do it all. My son was the last person I ever expected to drop the ball on. Maybe I spent too many overtime hours at work, or maybe I should've skipped some of those evenings that I stayed late at the hospital with my mother. Maybe it was just one of those things that happened when a boy doesn't have his father around. Whatever it was, I prayed that the move would bring change to his life for the better.

When Christmas day came, it was very weird to not have a tree up and have a nice big dinner. We barely had any pots or dishes out that weren't packed. One of the last things I packed was all our family photos. That had to be the saddest part of packing. It was very sad to see all the faces of the people we loved who were gone. I definitely sat and released a lot of tears for them. When I came across my baby pictures, I got really emotional. I used to keep the biggest smile on my face all the time. Now, I had to practice smiling before I took a picture. I know it will never be my place to question God about why I was given the life that I was living, but I always wondered why God took my nana away one month before I had my son. Why did my first real boyfriend choose to make me a baby momma and not his wife? Why did my grandparents move down south and leave me with my mother? Why did my mother, father, and his entire immediate family all have to die so soon? I promised myself to have happy thoughts the next time I sat down and looked at those photos.

By New Year's Eve, we were completely packed up with one bag open to dig out of for clean underwear. Jazz was already gone and getting situated in her own place, so we stayed home, watched the ball drop, and just enjoyed our last night watching TV because we had to turn the cable service off the next day. As I prepared for my last night ever in that apartment, I was happy, scared, and sad all at the same time. I never imagined that I would be living in another state, but it was either I was going to make it or I wasn't. The morning of the move was bittersweet. The time came to load up the rental truck and hit the road. We were all sad, but I knew deep down inside, that it was the best thing for us to do. We all deserved a brand-new start.

For the first month in our new place, we were like fish out of water. We had to learn where the locals shopped and how to get around. It didn't take us too long before we found out where the supermarket and fast food spots were located. I enjoyed my bus ride into the city for work because I always took the back-corner seat so I could take a nap. As we approached the spring of 2013, I started having problems with my left knee. At least two to three times a month, it would hurt so bad that I couldn't walk in the morning. It terrified me because I didn't want to end up having surgery again. Even though having surgery always felt like a vacation to me since I hated working, the reality of it all was that I couldn't afford to not go to work. My lack of finances was still a problem in my life. It was totally unacceptable to be unable to take time out to care for myself because of my lack of available funds. Being late on the rent and going to court was not an option anymore. Once I reached the point where I started missing work, I knew it was time to see Dr. Marx. We tried over the counter medicine, which didn't work for me. Then he sent me to do physical therapy, which strengthened my quads but didn't take the knee pain away.

One morning, I woke up in severe pain and couldn't stand up, so I hopped on one leg and went into my medicine cabinet. I found an old bottle of oxy with two pills left inside. The date on the bottle was expired, but I couldn't've cared less because I had every intention on still taking them. I figured the most that could happen would be that they wouldn't work. I knew for a fact that the expiration date on pills was just another way for these pharmaceutical companies to get you to order more. After laying down for fifteen minutes with an ice pack on my knee, the meds kicked in, and I fell asleep. I woke up two hours later with no pain, but my knee looked like I dragged it across a rug. It was the first time I ever saw freezer burn on skin. It was so bad that I had to use ointment and bandages for a week. The ice pack instructions specifically stated not to place the pack directly on skin, but I was so desperate to freeze out the pain that I took a chance.

After a few steroid injections that were unsuccessful, I had an MRI, and it showed that I had a meniscus tear. That was very shocking to hear since people who exercise or play sports usually got that type of injury. All I did was run my mouth. I knew that I couldn't avoid having surgery due to the amount of pain and problems I was having, so I decided to schedule it for mid-summer so I could financially prepare myself. I knew I wasn't going on any vacations because it just simply wasn't in my budget anyway. As the surgery date started approaching, things started getting messy at home again. One good thing going on was that KT received his first acceptance letter to SUNY Sullivan in New York. The time flew by so fast, and before I knew it, he was damn near an adult. Time waits for no one, and it kept catching me off guard. I didn't want my financial instabilities to be the reason why he couldn't go to school. I was determined to do whatever I had to do, and between a few good friends and my grandparents, we made it happen for him. The rest would be up to him once he got in. I wasn't too sure if he was mentally ready to go away just yet, but we wouldn't know until he went and tried.

Monty and I were not getting along. I didn't want to say things that would start an argument with him, but I had to let him know when something was bothering me. The problem was the main thing that usually bothered me always seemed to be women-related. Every time, I brought up an issue about a woman to him, he would get upset and say with lots of attitude that he wasn't doing anything. Then the next thing out of his mouth was always, "Where are you getting your information from?" As usual, social media was always behind the bullshit. It was always one or two females who just had to constantly comment on everything he posted like he was a damn celebrity. I knew he couldn't predict the petty shit they did, but he damn sure could've put them in their place for doing it. Instead, he would entertain it and tell me that I was overreacting.

Apparently, I was taking things way too serious and didn't realize it. Here I was thinking that I was just demanding to be respected.

When the day finally came for my surgery, I decided to go by myself so I could have some alone time. I just asked Monty to meet me in the recovery room so he could help me get home. My friend Tammy also came through to help me get home. During my recovery time at home, Monty was amazing to me. He took good care of me and my knee. Whenever I tried to get up and do things around the house, he would tell me, "Go sit your ass down somewhere before you fall," and I had no choice but to do just that. I was trying not to be annoying. I thought he was getting tired of me because sometimes, he would be in the living room with the music blasting and couldn't hear me if I was yelling for him. He'll never admit it, but I know he was drowning out my calls for help on purpose.

Chapter Twenty-Two

It was hard to sit around just doing leg workouts, but I had to follow the doctor's orders. I felt very awkward not cooking, grocery shopping, working, or doing laundry. I realized at that point that I didn't know how to relax. Relaxing was never an option for me. I felt guilty sitting around healing. My good friends came to visit me, gave me money, and brought me groceries. I felt truly blessed for all the love I received in my time of need. I healed a lot faster than I expected because of all the physical therapy I did before the surgery. That allowed me the opportunity to get back to work way before I imagined.

The time was fast approaching for KT to get ready to leave for school, and he didn't seem that excited. In this day and time, you have to support all positive choices that your kids make. He knew a lot of kids who were killed or in jail, so going to college was definitely a good thing. I could barely walk fast or sit with my knee bent for too long, but I had to get back to work so I could get my money right to keep him in school. Since the acceptance letter came so late in the summer, there was a lot of pressure on me, so I decided to reach out to his father to see if he would help out. I assumed that it wouldn't be a problem since he didn't pay child support. He was a very smart guy, so I felt that he would be on board to help the boy get out the hood for a while and get an education. Of course, he hit me with his favorite response…"Let me see what I can do." I really hated that bullshit. When you're a parent, you have to just do it.

By the time his father came through to help, he gave me less than half of what we discussed and missed all the deadlines to give it to me. Between being back to work and getting this college stuff sorted out, Monty and I were beefing again. All this stuff going on had my blood pressure out of control. I really couldn't afford to battle over our relationship at the time, so I tried to mentally prepare myself for whatever was going to happen. I had every intention on just letting shit happen with not an ounce of fight towards it. In the midst of everything, I received a call for a job interview near home, which shocked me because I never got call backs for jobs that paid decent. I decided to entertain the thought and set up the interview. The job was ten minutes away from home and paid more which would save me a few extra hundred dollars in travel expenses. The manager loved my resume and pretty much talked to me as if the job was already mine. I was very hesitant because I've never been a fan of trying out new things. Between the stress of trying to please well-to-do and privileged people, a long travel with a healing knee, and a desire to work close to home, I decided to accept the offer. I wasn't sure if this was a good idea, but I would never know unless I tried. Leaving my job was bittersweet because I spent almost ten years there, which was my longest commitment anywhere to anything. I also hated the thought of leaving my friends, but I knew we would see and speak to each other again if we were really friends. I figured that if all else failed with this new career venture, then I would just move on and find a new job like I always did.

While preparing for my big transition, I had to try to do as much physical therapy as possible on my knee. KT and his last-minute decision to attend school upstate was a relief because he wouldn't be too far away, but I was a little confused on why he chose a school upstate versus trying to attend a school in a much nicer area with warm weather or something down south. I guess he was still a little more attached to home than I thought. He loved to get away, just not for long. One thing for sure was that I had to help him while he was trying to do better in life. It was too easy for a young man to fall victim to the streets, so I had to do whatever it took to show him that I was willing to support his efforts. I thought to myself, this was definitely a good time to create some legal side hustles. I loved to write, so I decided to turn the things I wrote about secretly into a book. I figured selling books would be a good idea, but I didn't have the energy after work to sit down and really get serious about it. I was always too stressed out to focus on my personal goals, but I promised myself that I would keep writing things down in my notebook just in case the spirit hit me to really write a book. I needed a less stressful job with set hours so I could get home at a decent time and maybe have the energy to focus on my dreams. Every time I picked my notebook up to write, I would put that day's date next to it so I could see exactly when the last time I had written something was. I knew I wouldn't be making money off that anytime soon so I started researching waist trainers. I decided that I would buy one for myself and start wearing it because I can't sell a product that I don't even use. I need to believe in it before I can sell it to somebody else. Doing it any other way would feel like a scam. I wanted to also create a line of winter hats, but I didn't have the money to invest in the hats so I figured I would put that on the back burner for when the right time comes. Don't even get me started on my idea to open a laundromat or a daycare.

Monty and I were in a bit of an awkward place still. He was not happy with being in New Jersey and decided that he was leaving to go back to New York. I will never be the type of woman who tries to keep a man who didn't want to be kept, so I did the only thing left for me to do, which was to wish him well on his journey. At that point, I had too many different things going on anyway, and I needed to get focused before I had a nervous breakdown. He spent two days moving his belongings, and when he took the last of his stuff, I held back my tears, gave him a hug, and said goodbye. I am a strong woman, so I knew that I would be fine. I would never want him to stay with me knowing that he was spending his life full of regrets.

My baby, my mini me, my everything was leaving and hopefully ready for his new beginning. The day had finally arrived, and I was dreading it. The morning was a little hectic because he was up all night long hanging out with his friends and never went to sleep. He was acting like he didn't want to leave. His attitude took my sentimental feelings away and had me annoyed as hell. As we loaded up my homie Tammy's truck, the thought crossed my mind on how nice it would've been if both his parents could've taken him to school. Since Bee was never around, we all knew this event made no difference to him just like every other event that had passed. He seemed perfectly fine with missing out on everything. The most comforting thing about KT being at SUNY Sullivan was that he was just a bus ride away. As soon as we arrived at the campus, I got a nervous energy that I couldn't control. As we brought his belongings to the room, my anxiety started kicking into high gear. I started organizing his stuff in the room and telling his roommate where to put his stuff. I was losing control and couldn't get a grip. I was trying so bad not to cry that I had a huge lump in my throat. I had to keep telling myself that it was going to be okay because he wasn't in the streets hanging out anymore. There was literally nowhere to go out there. The school was like a small compound in the middle of an Amish town. I knew that part would bring me some peace.

Once we dropped off the last of his stuff, he walked us back to the truck. We gave long hugs, and I think he fought back tears too. I didn't know how to show my sensitive side in the public, so I took a long swallow, regained my composure, and said goodbye to my baby. I smiled as we pulled off because I knew he was off the streets officially. I felt blessed that at that moment, I wasn't leaving him behind in a hospital, jail, or cemetery. As soon as I got home to my now empty place, I sat down and cried a nice long cry. It was a cry of sadness, relief, confusion, and uncertainty. I was sad that my house was empty but relieved that my boy was safe.

I knew my friends weren't too far away, but I didn't want to bother them while they had their everyday lives to deal with too. I got up every day and went to work as if everything was okay. I never told anybody that I wasn't used to being apart from my son and worried about him doing the wrong things. All I knew at that point was that I had a new job starting soon, and my mind wasn't right.

About one week before my new job started, I got a call from Monty saying that he realized that he had made a mistake and wanted to come home. I had enough love and forgiveness in my heart to let him come back and to give it one last chance. Forgiveness was a big step in finding my maturity and growth as a woman. What better way to start with change then by starting within? We sat down and talked about how we could fix our relationship so we could have a better future together. We both knew and acknowledged our issues and agreed to work on them. Only time would tell if it would work out.

Chapter Twenty-Three

My last day at my job finally came, and it was so weird because I didn't know how to feel. One part of me was excited to work so close to home, but the other side was saying to stick with the bullshit I was already accustomed to dealing with. All my friends from work and I went out to eat and have drinks. We laughed a lot, and that made me feel better. My boss Dr. Green was around but not a part of the festivities at the table. I wasn't sure if he was mad at me or disappointed. He never expressed how he felt because he was hard on the outside just like me. I would hope that he understood that I was doing what I felt was in my best interest. It was because of bosses like him that I know how to multitask and work way above my own personal expectations, and I'll always be grateful for that. I took the following week off, and that concluded my time at the Hospital for Specialty Surgery. I needed a few days to work on my mental state and get adjusted to Monty being back home too.

My first day of my new job at University Hospital started, and it felt like the first day at a new school in a new town with no friends. After being introduced to the office staff, I got myself situated and just sat at my desk staring at the computer. I spent a decade working at the same place, and this new job made me feel like a fish out of water. I knew how to do my job as a medical secretary, but I had to learn how to make what I knew fit into the way they did things there. I loved learning new things, but my issue with that was my mind was so clouded with the stress in my personal life that I didn't feel like I was retaining the information the way I should have. I wasn't happy at all. I could sit for hours and not say two words. My coworkers were friendly for the most part, but at the same time, I wasn't really feeling it. I found out that the manager was very excited about me coming and spoke very highly of me. Apparently, she spoke so highly of me that it pissed off a few folks, so they were not digging me at all and throwing lots of shade my way. They all spoke to me, but then some of those same people would turn around and whisper about me. The funny part was when you whisper, the goal was for the person not to hear you, but I always did. Since my skin was tough, I didn't let it run me out of there. They weren't the ones signing my paycheck every two weeks, so I didn't need to confront anybody about it. It was just sad that a bunch of grown women formed an opinion about a stranger based off what somebody else said, and her info on me came from my resume and reference letter. The lady didn't know me personally. The job was compiled of just black and Spanish women, but all the shade seemed to come from the black women. It's a shame how black folks can't get along. I came to work literally just to work and not to deal with pettiness. The funny thing was they didn't know that my petty side was so extreme that I could probably teach a course in *Petty 101.* If my petty side would've been activated, I definitely would've given them a reason to dislike me.

Nobody wanted to get to know me, and they used my silence against me. I was silent because my personal life wasn't right, and I just wanted to make it through every day without a problem. I never brought my issues from home to work. I never took lunch breaks because I didn't need to sit with people who were talking about me. I never took lunch breaks at my old job either. I always ate my lunch at my desk while working so that was a hard habit to break, but they took that personal too. I did what I had to do every day, but at the same time, I was still stressed about my relationship with Monty and KT suddenly not liking school. Every other day, he was texting me complaining about everything from bugs outside to the cafeteria food and wanting to come home. He was literally stalking my life to the point where I gave in and let him come home to visit. The first time he came back, he had a good night sleep in his own bed, and the next day, he was out the door to see his friends. Not soon after that, I realized what his problem was. He missed his friends and wanted to come back home so bad that he couldn't focus on school. By the time the fall semester was over, he was put on academic probation, which meant that he couldn't stay on campus. There was absolutely nowhere to live off campus, so he had no choice but to come back home. I was so disappointed, but I had to accept that school might not have been for him at that moment. Again, it seemed like as soon as things began to look promising, something stupid had to happen to remind me that I wasn't allowed to have a perfect life or even a semi-functional one. Of course, I had to scrape up the money to pay my friend Darren to go get him and move his stuff back home. It was right before Christmas, and he already knew that holiday wasn't for him anymore, but even if it still was, he didn't deserve shit anyway.

When he got home, I told him that he didn't have the luxury to do anything, so he could either find a job or plan to go back to school for the fall semester. He was so happy to be home that he just said "Okay" and "Yes, Mommy" to whatever I said. I tried not stress over him messing up in school and tried to focus more on myself. I spent the next couple of months paying off bills and cleaning up my credit. I also convinced KT to take his SATs, so he could try to get into a better school. I knew he had the brains to take the test; I just needed him to recognize it for himself. When his scores came back, they were good enough for him to get accepted to Barry University in Miami. The only problem with that was he seemed to be afraid to go too far from home. As flattered as I was that he wanted to be nearby, I was disappointed that he didn't want to venture out into the world. He wanted to major in Sports Management, and Barry University seemed like the perfect place. Being the lunatic that I am, I went behind his back and applied to a four-year school near home on his behalf. It would take less than an hour to get there on the local buses. I even did his application essay. When the acceptance letter to William Patterson University came in the mail, he was so confused that all I could do was laugh, but he didn't want to go there either. He decided to look into a few more schools near home on his own. Once again, I wasn't quite sure how this was going to turn out, but I knew I had to support any positive moves he made. This time around, I planned to fade into the background and let him handle more of his own business. Sometimes, I got so caught up with helping out that I forgot where to draw the line and ended up doing everything myself. I've always had an overcompensating issue when it came to him. For everything that his father didn't do, I doubled up my efforts, so he never felt like he was lacking anything. I recognized my errors as he entered adulthood. The only thing that I felt I could do was pull back on my financial assistance and try giving more moral support. I figured it was better late than never. He was consuming a lot of my attention, and it distracted me from doing early planning for my 40th birthday that was coming up in a few months. I had no idea what I wanted to do, but I knew I had to do something.

I always told myself that I would be married by the time I turned 40. I figured by that age I should've known who I wanted to spend the rest of my life with. I didn't want to force Monty into marrying me, but I knew it was an issue that was not going to be kept under the rug anymore. I ended up having a small party for my birthday with some good friends and family. I danced so much in my heels that I sprained my ankle; that's what you call a damn good night in my book. Since my birthday is in June, I always tried to do something small with the intent of doing something bigger during the summer with my family, but something always prevented the trips from actually happening. The only trip that I always made happen was to go visit my grandparents in the south. That was the most important vacation that I could ever take because I was so blessed to still have them around. Even though they always got on my back about saving money for an emergency or a rainy day and losing weight, I knew it was coming from the heart. I knew they were telling me what I needed to hear, but boy oh boy, their delivery was brutal. They would flat out tell me to my face that they didn't know what the problem was, but I didn't lose any weight. I swear old people have no filter.

I didn't plan a trip for that summer because KT got a summer job in my department. Then he randomly decided during mid-summer that he wanted to go back to school upstate. Those were the things that happened when he was in charge of his own business. He knew how I hated poor planning, but he swore that he really wanted to go and would try his best to do well. If I didn't support his efforts in trying again, then I felt like I was a part of the problem if he failed. Once again, I jumped to the rescue and helped him with the application process but found out that it was too late to live on-campus. He wanted to entertain getting an off-campus apartment, so he started researching and talking with his friends and found one who was attending the same school. The parent of his friend was paying her portion of her rent, so I guess he was expecting the same from me. I told him that was my last extreme effort in trying to help him. If he messed that opportunity up, then he was totally on his own and would truly learn what the word 'struggle' meant.

He enrolled into SUNY Broome and decided again to major in Sports Studies. It was hard as hell financially for me to help him, but it also showed me that when it was all said and done, I could use that same money and put it away in my empty savings account. When he went away that time, I wasn't as sad as I was the first time. I was still worried, but I had to learn to let him be. As the fall season began, Monty and I were getting along very well. Things were looking up. Our quality time together was much better than it used to be. We had movie night, or sometimes, we just sat in the house playing old school music and partying hard all by ourselves.

Chapter Twenty-Four

We were turning into that fun loving couple we used to be. Everything at work started looking up too. My coworkers were getting nicer. I guess they finally realized that I wasn't there to be the enemy and that I just simply wanted to work close to home. One Saturday afternoon, I was getting dressed to do my normal errands, which consisted of going to the bank and the nail salon. After telling Monty where I was going, he told me he would come with me to keep me company. I always did my errands alone because I used it as another source of 'me' time, but I welcomed his company anyway.

As we were on our way to the nail salon, we stopped in a jewelry store so he could look at watches and inquire about getting new batteries for the ones we had. Somehow, we ended up looking at engagement rings in the back area of the store. They were beautiful, and they even had three-piece sets. The jeweler came to us and asked what we liked. We were both smiling and said, "No, thanks, we're just looking." He began to tell us about the prices and the special deals they had. We entertained the conversation, and he asked us again to pick out what sets we liked. When we did, he let us try the rings on. My ring didn't fit, but Monty's fit perfectly, like it was made for just for him.

"I can get you guys a really good deal."

"We'll be in touch," we said, taking his card.

We spent the next couple of hours analyzing where we were in life and if we really wanted to stay together. At that very moment, we decided to get married. I know that wasn't the traditional way of getting engaged, but I didn't have time to try to figure out how to be traditional. My life was closer to being ratchet if anything else. I was very happy and scared at the same time. For a few weeks, I kept double-checking with him to make sure that he was serious because we had to inform our families. We decided to just initially tell his mother and my grandparents. Once we told them, we knew the information would spread to the rest of the family. We picked a date, and he came up with the color scheme that would reflect the fall season. We were slowly releasing the news to our people. In the meantime, I was researching venues and looking at dresses. Together we agreed that we would only invite the people who had been around the time that were together. It made no sense to invite someone who didn't know either one of us. The only default invites would go out to our families.

We didn't have one penny set aside for the wedding, but that gave us more reason to make it small and meaningful. Spending thousands of dollars wasn't going to prove our love for each other. When you see all the celebrities who have had lavish weddings getting divorced, that proves my point. I always heard women say how stressful wedding planning was. I heard stories about how people always went over budget and spent years paying that debt off. I guess that wouldn't be my issue because I had no money to start out with. I didn't plan on applying for any lines of credit or borrowing from anyone either. If we couldn't pay straight up cash for something, then we just wouldn't be having it. I was not going to be the next horror story with financial woes for a one-day event. Every time I called a venue and they asked what event I was having, the price always skyrocketed. The wedding business was booming and something to consider in the future for a side hustle. Every day when I came home from work, I was looking at wedding dresses, and of course, that was a headache. Monty wasn't really into the wedding planning and pretty much went with whatever I wanted to do. I noticed that most men didn't bother with the planning part of things, and that bothered me a little. It made me wonder if the whole ceremony thing was even worth it; maybe we should have just go down to City Hall and then have a party after, but then I started thinking that I was cheating my grandparents and his mother out of the experience of the wedding. This whole thing was raising my blood pressure and was no longer fun. I started to wonder if we should've just left the country and got married on a beach with a few close people in attendance. I would sit at my computer for hours tripping over what to do and how to do it while Monty sat on the couch just watching me go crazy. I created a spreadsheet with our guest list and that kept changing because some people had passed away, then there were the people who I forgot about, and last but not least, I couldn't forget about the default relatives who had to be invited or else Grandma would get upset. Monty kept telling me that he was down for whatever I wanted to do. We at least knew we wanted to get married a year later around the fall of 2015, but everything else was up in the air. In the meantime, Grandma and Grandpa already bought their outfits for the ceremony, so that meant we had to be more organized because my grandma would never let me hear the end of it if she didn't get to wear her suit with the hat to match. If all else failed, we would push the time back for the special event because it had to be right. I just prayed to God that nothing went wrong and we end up backing out of it or breaking up. I planned to keep the faith. We were all overdue for a happy ending.

I will never understand why life has dealt me the hand that it has, but I have accepted all of these things as lessons to learn from. I'm still learning how to not get upset when I don't like what someone says. I'm taking things one day at a time, and that seems to work well for me. I respect people more now for who they really are, and I don't knock them or try to change them. Everybody has a position that they play at this time in my life, and whenever necessary, I will just switch their position based on how they react towards me. I know who means well and who's fake. There are a lot of people who I love from a distance. When it comes to work, instead of spending my entire work days aggravated that I have to be there, I've been trying to consider it the ladder that I'm climbing to reach my own personal goals. I spend the hours of 8:30 a.m.-4:30 p.m. helping others build their dreams. Now, I dedicate my life after work to building my own dreams. I also use the fact that I work for Dr. Osula who is a black female surgeon as a key part of my personal motivation. I respect the fact that I am able to keep waking up every morning even though I am cranky as hell. I'm truly grateful, and I know that means God knows my work isn't done on this earth yet, and if you woke up today, neither is yours. I owe it to myself to never let anyone or anything keep me from reaching my full potential. I feel like I had a late start in life, but I guess it's better late than never. While I work on myself, I feel like it's now my civic duty to help others recognize when they have a gift and are not using it. I want to see all the people around me do well and living a meaningful life. It's okay if you try something for the first time and it doesn't work out. I've put myself in quite a few financial jams because I wanted to jump out the window on a leap of faith. There were some ideas and ventures that I wanted to tap into, and I knew there was never going to be a "right time", so I used money I really didn't have to work on those opportunities for a better life. I haven't struck gold yet or hit the jackpot, but I'm definitely more optimistic than ever before and a lot wiser when it comes to tapping into my potential. Sometimes, I can sit in front of the computer for hours on the internet, using it to research and expand my thought process on how to build my future with the hopes of creating wealth. You will respect yourself more if you don't give up. The worst life we can all live is a life full of regrets. We must chase our dreams, follow our hearts, and go after what we want. Some of us may have the opportunity to be in history books for the children of our future, so let's make it be for something good. We can all respect that in an imperfect world, we may not always get it right, but at least, we're trying.

Made in the USA
Columbia, SC
13 November 2017